ORIENTAL LIBRARIES OF INDIA IN INTERNET AGE

ORIENTAL LIBRARIES OF INDIA IN INTERNET AGE

Faisal Mustafa

Oriental Libraries of India in Internet Age

ISBN : 978-81-8205-949-6

Published in 2013 in India by
Kalpaz Publications
C-30, Satyawati Nagar,
Delhi - 110052
E-mail: kalpaz@hotmail.com

Laser Type Setting : Rajender Vashist, Delhi
Printed at : Chawla Offset Printers, Delhi

Dedicated to
My Parents

Contents

Foreword

According to the Fourth Annual Report of the National Mission for Manuscripts "India is perhaps one of the biggest manuscripts reserves in the world." A random survey of a non-descript district of Uttar Pradesh, Unnao, yielded 2,500 manuscripts, including a *Mahabharata* manuscript weighing one quintal and a ten meter long *Quran*. Up to February 2009, the Mission had collected information for existence of 2, 14, 000 manuscripts in the country. It is unfortunate that the present efforts at the preservation and conservation of the nation's cultural assets in had to wait for half a century. We don't know the number of valuable manuscripts which had perished before the Mission was initiated in 2003. Of course, the National Archives of India had initiated a scheme, in the seventies of the last century, for providing funds and some guidance for conservation and cataloguing of manuscripts to institutions having manuscripts and other archival materials. The Mission has taken up a very challenging job of identification, preservation and providing access to these valuable basic sources of scholarship.

Before the arrival of the British as occupation power, India had libraries with most of the ruling houses and princely states in the country. Besides, temples, *maths*, *dargahs* of Sufi saints also had libraries for the devotees since these places also functioned as seats of learning. According to Sir Jadu Nath Sarkar, the eminent historian of the medieval Indian history, The Imperial Library of the Mughals possessed fine examples of calligraphy and illumination such as had no rivals in the East. De Laet in his book *The Empire of the Great Mughal* records that Akbar's Library at his death consisted of 24,000 volumes ... In the later days of the Mughals a number of rare materials of the Imperial Library found their way to Awadh library at Lucknow. Sprenger, who was engaged to prepare a catalogue of the library, has confirmed having seen 10,000 books in the library. The first volume of his catalogue was published in1854 from Calcutta.

Unfortunately the British officers of the early days, who had virtually occupied the country even before 1857, had scant respect for the Indian cultural heritages. Lord Curzon is on record that William Bentinck, a former Governor General, wanted to pull down the Taj for selling its marbles. Lord Wellesley was pulled up for delaying transfer of the library of Tipu Sultan to England. On the death of Wajid Ali Shah, his library was loaded in a carriage and taken away by a British officer. During the period of turmoil after the defeat of forces fighting for Bahadur Shah Zafar in 1857, the remaining collection at the Lal Qila was looted by the British forces. According to Sir Jadu Nath, the Nawab of Rampur whose forces had sided with the British, offered one rupee for each manuscript that his sepoys brought to him. The collection thus acquired became the basic collection for the now well known Rampur Raza Library. The founders of the four world known manuscript libraries of India, namely the Khuda Baksh Public Library, Patna, Rampur Raza Library, Salar Jung Museum, Hyderabad and Tanjore Maharaja Sarfoji's Saraswati Mahal Library, Thanjavur, played a major role in arresting the outward flow of our valuable cultural assets.

The two Britishers, to whom we must pay our respects for protecting our cultural assets, are William Jones, who, in 1784, established The Asiatic Society in Calcutta, and Lord Curzon, the Viceroy and Governor General of India, who established the Archeological Survey of India and also founded the Imperial Library in 1903.

The Asiatic Society, the oldest socieiy by this name in the world, is now an important centre for Indic Studies.

The Imperial Library developed and was christened as The National Library of India in 1949 and but for the Archaeological Survey, all our world famous monuments would have gone the way the famous Mughal bath at the Agra Fort which was dismantled and the marble were sold out in pre Curzon period.

The Mission through its nation wide survey has been successful in identifying almost half of the number it aims at achieving at the close of the project. The Mission has already digitized about 55,000 manuscripts. It has also come to light that Manuscripts are not available only in oriental libraries. Old universities such as Aligarh, Banaras and Calcutta without being oriental libraries also posses' collection of rare books and manuscripts. Thus the country is not poor in resources for study and research in Indic subjects. It is poor in information about their existence and about facilities available for their use.

The two basic requirements for successful utilization of the resources are:

(a) Dissemination of information about the libraries, archives and research centres, regarding their, collection, access facilities and services, etc. and

(b) Extent of preservation and conservation and digitsation facilities for the available assets that are being provided in these libraries.

The National Mission for Manuscript has included the following points also among its objectives:

1. Survey, document and catalogue Indian manuscripts wherever they be and compile a national data base,

2. Facilitate conservation and preservation of manuscript through training awareness building and financial support,

3. Provide ready access to these manuscripts through digitization and publication.

Till such time as the IGNCA achieves these objectives, descriptive accounts of libraries, archives and research centres possessing manuscripts and archival records will go a long way in helping the research community in planning its research programme. The book prepared by Dr. Faisal Mustafa is a welcome attempt as a guide for research scholars looking for the information about these centres. He has done well to throw light on the state of digitization being carried out in these libraries under the guidance of the IGNCA.

New Delhi
12th March, 2012

Shahabuddin Ansari
Ex-University Librarian
Dr. Zakir Husain Library
Jamia Millia Islamia
New Delhi

Acknowledgments

At the beginning, I would like to copiously thank Janab Shahabuddin Ansari, Ex-University Librarian, Dr. Zakir Husain Library, Jamia Millia Islamia, New Delhi, who with pleasure accede to my request to write a 'Foreword' for this work. In connection with this work, I happened to meet and discuss with a large number of individuals, in person. I sincerely thank the librarians, directors, secrateries and incharges of the the select Libraries/Institutions who have spared their valuable time, offerd guidance and provided necessary data, which has gone into this work. At the same time, I am also thankful to employees of the select libraries/ institutions for their timely support. A few of them have also provided me relevant data through electronic mail. I am also thankful to them.

My sincere thanks are also due to my Library collegues at MANUU College of Teacher Education, Srinagar, J&K for providing motivation and a scholarly help througout the period in which I was busy in writing this Script. Thanks is also due to my former Principal at MANUU College of Teacher Education, Srinagar, J&K, Prof. Mohammad Iqbal Nazki, who always wanted me to do some academic work in my own field. His scholarly guidance accompanied with mentoring tendency has always encouraged me to do something on the lines. I am also thankful to my colleuges at HMS Central Library, Jamia Hamdard, New Delhi and School of Education and Training, MANUU for their valuable help in the content development of this Book.

Last but not the least; I would like to convey my sincere thanks to my brother and mentor Prof. Khurram Mustafa,

Head, Department of Computer Science, JMI, New Delhi, for shaping me academically at every stage. I am also thankful to my wife Mrs. Samina Rehman and my son Master Musub Faruqi for their silent help, encouragement and giving their precious time to me for this noble cause. I am also thankful to my parents, brothers, sisters, brother in laws, sister in laws and their children and all friends for their tiring support, silent help and encouragements. I might have neglected some of my duties towards them but they never complaint of it.

July 2012 **Faisal Mustafa**

Abbreviations

A.D.	:	Anno Domini
A.H.	:	After Hegira
APGOMLRI	:	Andhra Pradesh Government Oriental Manuscripts Library and Research Institute
APSCL	:	Andhra Pradesh State Central Library
ASB	:	Asiatic Society of Bombay
ASL	:	Asiatic Society Library
ASM	:	Asiatic Society of Mumbai
BORI	:	Bhandarker Oriental Research Institute
CIBS	:	Central Institute of Budhist Studies
CD	:	Compact Disc
CPL	:	Connemara Public Library
DL	:	Digital Library
DLI	:	Digital Library of India
DMSA	:	Darul Musannefeen Shibli Academy
DTP	:	Desk Top Printing
DUNU	:	Darul Uloom Nadvatul Ulama
GOMLRC	:	Government Oriental Manuscripts Library and Research Centre
HPMSL	:	Hazrat Pir Mohammad Shah Library
ICT	:	Information and Communications Technology
IGNCA	:	Indira Gandhi National Centre for Arts
IIIT	:	International Institute of Information Technology
INTACH	:	Indian National Trust for Arts and Cultural Heritage

IOL	:	Indian Oriental Libraries
KBOPL	:	Khuda Bakhsh Oriental Public Library
LAN	:	Local Area Network
LC	:	Library of Congress
LTWA	:	Library of Tibetan Works and Archives
MAAPRI	:	Maulana Azad Arabic and Persian Research Institute
MANUU	:	Maulana Azad National Urdu University
MARC	:	MAchine Readable Catalogue
MCC	:	Manuscript Conservation Centre
MoU	:	Memorandum of Understanding
MPC	:	Manuscript Partner Centre
MRC	:	Manuscript Resource Centre
Mss.	:	Manuscript
NAMMAMI	:	National Mission for Manuscripts
NIC	:	National Informatics Centre
NICNET	:	National Informatics Centre NETwork
NKC	:	National Knowledge Commission
NL	:	National Library
NGO	:	Non Government Organisation
OL	:	Oriental Library
OPAC	:	Online Public Access Catalogue
RAS	:	Royal Asiatic Society
RRL	:	Rampur Raza Library
SDKJORI	:	Shri D.K. Jain Oriental Research Institute
SJML	:	Salar Jung Museum and Library
SORI	:	Scindia Oriental Research Institute
TM	:	Tawang Monastry
TMSSML	:	Thanjavor Maharaja Saraswati Mahal Library
UN	:	United Nations
UNESCO	:	United Nations Educational Scientific and Cultural Organisations

1

Introduction

The precise and universally accepted definition of oriental libraries does not exist. Its source word "orient" itself, perhaps, not defined very clearly in any context. But, in the ongoing discussions as well as expediency of the readers, there is always a need to define a term which is being so popularly used in India and elsewhere. The term "orient" means eastern oppose to word "occident" of similar nature which means western, however, these are dictionary meaning of the said terms. The related terms "oriental" and "orientalist" comes from the word orient. Oriental in its most literal form means of or from the orient, as opposed to occidental meaning from the occident. In more general usage, oriental means of or from the east, and has been applied as an adjective to objects, places and the people. One of the meanings of the word 'oriental' in the Oxford Dictionary is:

"Belonging to or found in or characteristics of the countries or regions lying in the East of the mediterannean or the ancient Roman Empire; belonging to South-Western Asia or Asiatic countries generally."

The oriental meaning whatever belongs to east whether language, literature, culture or folklore. It includes everything which happens to be part and parcel of the eastern people. Those, who being an occidental, study the language, literature or culture associated with eastern societies, are technically known as 'Orientalists'.

Therefore, a precise definition of an 'Oriental Library' is the one which contains precious information and knowledge about the oriental language, literature or culture or it belongs to eastern world. Within this framework, any kind of library having vast collections of oriental documents is known as an Oriental Library.

Though, Narinder Kumar Sharma in his paper 'Oriental Libraries in India' defined the oriental libraries in the following words:

"When used as qualifier to libraries the composite term "Oriental Libraries" means the libraries that have the literature pertaining to oriental studies and languages; the subjects have their origin in the orient or deal with the classical languages of the orient. The present oriental libraries, even if started as repositories of oriental literature with a solitary function of preservation, have stopped short of extending their activities to areas of the collection and selection of reading materials appropriate for an oriental library; preservation of reading materials for posterity, and; the organisation of reading materials for modern library services."

There are, at least, three types of oriental libraries exist in India e.g. public, academic and special. Most of the public libraries in India have specialization in oriental collections. Manuscript libraries and research centres having emphasis on oriental languages, literature, and culture are also come under the category of oriental libraries. Apart from these public libraries, a few libraries are per se considered as oriental libraries. A number of academic and special libraries of India hold a vast number of books and manuscripts in oriental languages and literature and these, too, are considered as oriental libraries.

There are a number of famous libraries focused in oriental languages and literature collections in India. The various important roles of these libraries not only include 'providing assistance to the research scholars and students' but also preserving the infrequent printed documents and manuscripts of the earlier period for the future use. There are plenty of libraries those contain a very good collection in one or another oriental languages such as Hindi, Urdu, Bengali, Tamil, Telugu, Persian, Arabic, Sanskrit, Kannada, etc. yet, most of the collections in these libraries appear to be utmost importance due to following:

- Growth of collection in such areas i.e. oriental language, literature and culture is getting confined to acquitting ancient manuscript from different sources.
- Preservation modes and technologies for such a collection are still in infancy.
- Such oriental collections preserve the history, culture and civilization particularly of ancient and medieval period India in the form of primary and secondary sources of information.
- Trends of developing collection, by default, in the oriental languages and literature are diminishing and are largely overtaken by English.
- There is strong demand for primary literature for fundamental research in history, language and culture.
- The treasures of rare manuscripts and old printed documents having vast and invaluable knowledge are diminishing day by day.

There appears little apprehensiveness that developments and civilization during ancient and medieval period India is utmost important not only from the perspective of academics but also from the perspectives of minorities-social and contemporary issues. A few of the prominent organisations, having a good collection of oriental languages and literature in Urdu, Arabic, Persian, Sanskrit, Telugu etc. includes the names: Khuda Bakhsh Oriental Public Library, Patna, Rampur Raza Library, Rampur, National Library of India, Kolkata, Andhra Pradesh Government Oriental Manuscripts Library and Research Institute, Hyderabad, The Asiatic Society Libraries at Kolkata and Mumbai, Maulana Abul Kalam Azad Arabic and Persian Research Institute, Tonk, Salar Jung Museum and Library, Hyderabad, Maharaja Serfoji's Saraswati Mahal Library, Thanjavur, The Connemara Public Library, Chennai,

Bhandarkar Oriental Research Institute, Pune, Central Institute of Buddhist Studies, Leh, Adyar Library and Research Centre, Chennai, Government Manuscript Library, Allahabad and so on.

The Context

There are escalating demands for digital access to information resources. This helps users to get the required information in a very short time. A single copy can be mounted on a server, and this can be viewed and downloaded by a large number of users, simultaneously, and from any location in the world. The apparent advantage of such a system is that it liberates the document from the constraints of traditional access methods. Due to the number of advantages, a large number of institutions have got their collections either digitized or in the process of digitization. Therefore, it is necessary and feasible to study the progress pattern of few important oriental libraries of India as these are planning to disseminate their collections content through the help of automation and digitization techniques. The libraries have adopted various techniques of digitizing their collection for better dissemination of knowledge contained in their documents. It is also need of the hour to make use of Information and Communications Technology (ICT) for proper and adequate usage of documents by multiple kinds of users. With the advent of innovative Information and Communications Technologies (ICT), the preservation of books, periodicals, manuscripts, and even traditional media such as palm leaves, has become easier. Preserving culture and social history of a country is thus of prime importance for any culture entering the digital age. India has one of the oldest and largest collections of manuscripts in the world mostly formed in oriental languages and scripts. Today, most of the libraries/ institutes in the country have realized the in-built merits of digitization and are involved in setting up of digital libraries. The global access and utilization of rare manuscripts and significant documents are one of the most important aims of a reputed public library. Through automation and digitization, these organizations are trying their level best to survive in the age of Internet.

Scope of the work

The topic of the book is "Oriental Libraries of India in Internet Age". India has a long tradition of libraries through the ages. There are a very large number of public libraries which have specialization in oriental collections. Still, these libraries serve as research repositories for the growth and development of the knowledge. This study, therefore, has been framed to investigate the establishment, collections, preservation and modernization of libraries to cope with the era of information technology. These libraries being repositories of important documents of older times and rare manuscripts also serve as basis for fundamental research. There is also need to emphasize its importance to those who are concerned with the historical research in different areas. The collection of manuscripts preserved in these libraries is not only pride of any nation but also a primary source of information. The accessibility of these manuscripts is diminishing because these have not been provided a sound platform through which world populace identify and utilize it. There are always copyright problems with these documents which are also responsible factors for its less usage.

The study has been taken up to accomplish the following objectives:

(i) To identify major public libraries/repositories of India possessing a very strong collection in oriental languages, literature and culture.

(ii) To evaluate the policy of collection development and preservation techniques for manuscripts and rare documents.

(iii) To evaluate the present situation of various modernization techniques being used in these libraries.

(iv) To suggest what can be done to modernize these libraries.

(v) To recognize the development pattern with respect of their modernization.

The study started with the hypothesis that a good number of oriental public libraries in India which are in their infancy as far as digitization of their collections are concerned. Though, most of these institutions have already started digitizing their documents one or other way. Moreover, most of the select institutes have their own websites and they have at least started their automation process, being the first phase of modernization to cope with drastic changes taking place due to growth and development of Information and Communications Technology (ICT).

The study is limited to the literature available on the Internet whether in the form of website of the concerned institution or any other online format as well as printed documents about each oriental libraries of India. The author has delimited his study and confined it to only twenty major organisations which possess very strong collection of oriental documents in the form of printed books and manuscripts. The author has tried his level best to have a room for various kinds of organizations in his study in terms of languages, cultures and religions prevalent in India. The very selection of organizations itself provides unbiased approach and scholarly insights while going through it. Accordingly, the select organizations have been placed in a general alphabetical order for convenience of the readers. National Mission for Manuscripts has also taken into consideration due to its sturdy efforts in the preservation and digitization of Indian oriental documents despite the fact that basically it is dealing with manuscripts. As, its contribution is not only limited to libraries and information centers but it also reached to temples, mosques, mutts, monasteries and personal collections for the search of Indian heritage documents.

Websites of different institutions are visited for collecting latest and most relevant information as to whether they have started computerization/ automation and digitization of their invaluable collections or not and also to identify whether they are planning to do so. Information relevant to the present study has been collected from their websites apart from other printed sources.

2

Present Situation of Indian Oriental Libraries (IOL)

Introduction

In India, there is a long tradition of libraries having emphasis on the collection in oriental languages and literature. The primary purpose of these kinds of libraries has to preserve the cultural heritage in the form of books and manuscripts. These libraries, since very long period have been serving as repositories of our invaluable cultural heritage which are building blocks of our future historical and fundamental research. The existing states of these Indian libraries/ organisations differ from region to region as well as their organisational structure accompanied with the status of their parent institutions. Few of these are directly functioning under the control of central government, others are in the patronage of state governments and few are autonomous in nature. Though, quality of collections is some extent similar but the situation differs from libraries to libraries. Few of these have already started digitization of their precious collections, others are just started automation but a small number of libraries are lagging behind in comparison to others.

Akin to libraries anywhere in the world, public and private funds are needed to build, safeguard and preserve their books and manuscripts. The documentary heritage in India is also in short supply of funds, leading to stagnation, thefts and deterioration of existing collections. Due to importance attached with these libraries accompanied with its access are most important aspects of concern for each and everyone. These libraries need special attention to study and a systematic plan for familiarizing these treasures of knowledge worldwide. These libraries preserve those collections on which our future historical research depend upon. There is also an urgent need to make available accurate statistical data about their collections of printed books as well as manuscripts. At the same time, these libraries, should display language wise break up of their printed books and manuscripts collection for convenience of the scholars and researchers. Hence, the disparity about the same will be reduced for a better cause.

Automation is a unique technique to provide bibliographic information about a particular document through online format. It contains every aspects of the library whether housekeeping operations, administrative ones or user based. But, one of the most important aspects dealt in automation is to provide online user friendly catalogue. These catalogues are same in respect of format to manual catalogues and serves same purpose but due to its online format it serves so many added functions as compare to manual catalogues. The most important feature of these catalogues lies in its online and global access, if provided on the Internet. Most of Indian libraries have started automation and computerization work in early 1990s irrespective of academic, special or public libraries. Though, most of these libraries have not displayed their Online Public Access Catalogue (OPAC) on their particular website.

Digitization means acquiring, converting, storing and providing information in a computer format that is standardized, organised and available on demand from common system. Manuscripts and other rare printed documents are converted into compressed digital formats with specialized scanners or any other techniques and stored systematically for future reference. It is a new technique through which documents are available in electronic format either on-line or off-line. But, the essence of digitization only obtained when thought content of the documents should be made available on-line.

The Wikipedia, the free encyclopaedia defines the term digital library in following manner:

"A digital library is a library in which collections are stored in digital formats (as opposed to print, microform, or other media) and accessible by computers. The digital content may be stored locally, or accessed remotely via computer networks. Whereas the DELOS Digital Library Reference Model[2] defines a digital library as:

"An organization, which might be virtual, that comprehensively collects, manages and preserves for the long term rich digital content, and offers to its user communities specialized functionality on that content, of measurable quality and according to codified policies."

A distinction is often made between content that was created in a digital format, known as born-digital, and information that has been converted from a physical medium, e.g., paper. The term hybrid library is sometimes used for libraries that have both physical collections and digital collections. For example, American Memory is a digital library within the Library of Congress. Most of Indian academic, special and public libraries are example of these kinds of libraries.

The global access of the thought content is one of the most important features of a digital library. It will break all the geographical boundaries throughout the world. Therefore, every library of the world is now doing sturdy effort in this direction. The thought content of manuscripts and printed documents should be digitized due to its strong demand globally. Traditional knowledge, presently available amongst indigenous people in folklore or other forms, is now being explored and documented. The digitization of century-old publications and rare documents is being carried out in different institutions across this sub-region to preserve them and make them accessible through networks of digital archives.

There are various options available for digitization of reading material. The re-typing is not possible in case of manuscripts. Scanning is the only possibility in case of manuscripts. It is nothing more than a picture of printed page in digital form. Digital imaging technology convert manuscripts into digital images and can be made available over electronic networks - a digital image is composed of set of pixels. The text can be retrieved, printed and modified using appropriate software. The scanning of manuscripts using computer image scanner is done carefully due to variations in text and colour and images.

Indian libraries are also trying their level best to cope with this situation. It is true that, initially, the digitization work has started in academic and scientific libraries, but, now public and oriental libraries of India have also started digitization with support of government of India and other agencies. The trends are changing in most of the public libraries of India. The National Mission of Manuscripts is also helping the public libraries to transform their rare manuscripts and valuable printed documents into digital format for better and global access. Digitization of manuscripts and rare printed volumes as means of protecting and documenting textual heritage has emerged as an important field in recent times. With the advancement of Information Technology, digitization promises documentation and preservation of original texts, facilitating at the same time, greater access for scholars and researchers. The following are main objectives of digitizing manuscripts and rare printed volumes:

- Preservation of original documents for posterity
- Promotion of access and usage of scholars and researchers, without tempering with original copies
- Creation of a digital database of Indian manuscripts and rare printed documents, and
- Creation of standards and procedures for digitization of manuscripts and rare printed documents.

In the following passages, an attempt has been made to highlight the achievement made by the twenty chosen oriental libraries in the country in the direction of modernization, automation and digitization of their invaluable printed documents and rare manuscripts.

The present state of these libraries of India varies with their geographical boundaries. Yet, they have some common merits.In the following passages, a brief description of each library including their establishment, growth, collection development, manuscript preservation, publications, automation, digitization initiatives etc have been highlighted.

Andhra Pradesh Government Oriental Manuscripts Library and Research Institute, Hyderabad

2. Andhra Pradesh government Oriental Manuscripts Library and Research Institute, Hyderabad

Profile of the Library

The Andhra Pradesh Government Oriental Manuscripts Library and Research Institute was established in the Andhra Pradesh State Archives Department in 1967 with a view to salvaging the valuable and rare manuscripts in the State and making tham available to scholars. In 1975, it was granted an independent directorate under the Department of Education to develop the manuscripts library as an advanced research institute. Now, it is located in a nice building at Osmania University Campus, Hyderabad. The main objectives of the Institute are as follows:

- To collect and preserves the manuscripts for posterity
- To provide research facilities to scholars and other stakeholders
- To create awareness about the importance of the Institute among the scholars, writers and general users by organizing exhibitions, seminars, lectures, discussion and awareness rallies
- Supply of xerox copies of manuscripts and microfilms to the scholars
- Publishing the rare and unpublished manuscripts in a phased programme
- Editing of rare manuscripts.

The Institute through the three and half decades of its existence took pains to collect rare manuscripts from private individuals and philanthropic organisations. Some of the manuscripts are also purchased on the basis of recommendations made by the Expert Committee. The major organisations and individuals who donated books and manuscripts to this Institute are:

- Andhra Pradesh State Central Library: 17,124
- Sri Venkateshwara Oriental Research Institute, Tirupati: 332
- Zilla Granthalaya Samstha, Adilabad: 77
- Zilla Granthalaya Samstha, Medak: 14.

The greatest manuscript in this Library is world's biggest manuscript written by a single person Swamy Ranganathacharya over a period of thirty five years. The greatest of all his works is Encyclopedia Lexicon in Sanskrit. This work was started in 1865.[1]

Publications

Publications of rare and unpublished manuscripts are also another important objective as well as function of the Institute. It has an active policy of printing books from its own manuscripts collection as facsimile edition, special edition and annotated editions. Institute has so far printed around 65 books in English, Telugu, Persian and Urdu Languages. The Institute has an ambitious plan to publish all the rare manuscripts facsimile editions for which it is seeking collaborations from other organizations and institutes. The Institute has already published its Descriptive Catalogue of Telugu manuscripts in three volumes.[2]

Lists of some of the important descriptive catalogues and books already printed by the Institute are as follows:

1. A descriptive catalogue of Urdu manuscripts (Poetry). Compiled by Rafat Rizwana. Vols.1, APGOMLRI, Hyderabad,1988
2. A descriptive catalogue of Urdu manuscripts (Poetry). Compiled by Rafat Rizwana. Vols.2, APGOMLRI, Hyderabad,1994
3. Fihrist Mashruh Baaz Kutub Nafsiyah Qalmiyah Makhzoon Kutubkhana Asafiya Sarker-e-Aali. Vol.2. Darut Taba Sarkar-e-Aali, Hyderbad, 1357 A.H.
4. Hand Book of Andhra Pradesh Government Oriental Manuscripts Library and Research Institute. Compiled by V.V.L. Narsimha Rao and V.Sarala Kumari. APGOMLRI, Hyderabad, 1988.
5. Alphabetical subject wise Index of Telugu manuscripts available in APGOMLRI, Hyderabad (Telugu). Compiled by K. Vittal Reddy and K.S. Stayanarayana
6. Alphabetical subject wise Index of Telugu manuscripts available in APGOMLRI, Hyderabad (Telugu). Compiled by D.K. Srinivasachary and K.V. Rama Sastry
7. Alphabetical subject wise Index of Urdu manuscripts available in APGOMLRI, Hyderabad (English). Compiled by Mir Karamat Ali.
8. Descriptive catalogue of Telugu manuscripts (Telugu). Vols.3. Compiled by K.Vittal Reddy
9. Engula Veera Swamy's Journal (English Prose)

10. Sri Virupksha-Sri Rama Copper Plate inscriptions
11. Indumathi Parinayamu (Telugu Poetry)
12. Bhargava Puranamu (Telugu Poetry)
13. Sita Kalyanamu(Telugu)
14. Taraka Brahma Rajeeyamu (Telugu)
15. Sringara Padamulu (Telugu)
16. Naradeeya Puranumu (Telugu)
17. Kavi Chintamani (Telugu)
18. Udayanodayamu and Vanamali Vilasamu (Telugu)
19. Arsha Kutumbamu (Telugu)
20. Vajragiri Narsimha Satakamu (Telugu)
21. Ramarajavatamsa Satalkamu(Telugu)
22. Yogasakta Parinayamu(Telugu)
23. Sri Geeta Govindam-Sri Geeta Sankaram(Sanskirit in Telugu Script)
24. Alankara Makarandah (Sanskrit)
25. Vaikrita Chandrika (Sanskirit)
26. Alankara Makarandah (Sanskirit)
27. Minhaj-ur-Raza (Arabic)
28. Tarikh-i-Adil Shahi (Persian)
29. Bayaz-l-Chandulal (Persian)
30. Makatib-l-Abdulah Qutubshah (Persian)
31. Tarikh-Asafjahi (English)
32. Nasikatpuran trnaslated from Sanskrit to Urdu
33. Tarikh-l-Feroz Shahi (Urdu)
34. Mustalhat-e-Thaggi (Urdu)
35. Khutut-e-Mir Aalam (Urdu)
36. Al-Nazmur-Durar-wal-Marjan (Arabic)
37. Radha Vamseedhara Vilas Natak(Hindi)
38. Nahush (Hindi)

Renowned Manuscripts

The A.P Government Oriental Manuscripts Library and Research Institute, at present have a rich and magnificent collection of above twenty four thousands manuscripts in sixteen languages. The major collection of manuscripts comprises of palm-leaf and handmade paper in Sanskrit, Arabic, Persian, Pushto, Telugu, Kannada, Marathi, Urdu, Hindi, Oriya, and Sindhi languages. These manuscripts are related to forty seven subjects such as Vedas. Upanishads, Puranas, Agamas, Dharma,Shasthras, Grammar, Prosody, Music, Alankarasastra, Tantrasastras, Ayurveda, Kavyas, Holy Quran and Quranic Exegesis, Hadis, Fiqh, History, Unani Medicine, Astrology and Dictionaries. There are many illustrated manuscripts with rare artistic excellence and some of them are specimens of exceptionally brilliant calligraphy. These manuscripts provide knowledge about the realities and literary heritage, contemporary histories and genealogies. The manuscripts give us contemporary data about the socio-religious milieu. During the forty years of its exit stance, the Library has enriched thousand of scholars with rare glimpses of the past and gradually it has emerged as one of the richest repository of the manuscripts in the South India.

The Insitute has also received more than 17,060 valuable and rare manuscripts dating back to 5th and 6th centuries from the Andhra Pradesh State Central Library, Hyderabad in the year 1967.

Few of its rarest among rare manuscripts titles is worthy to mention here which is now in the custody of Andhra Pradesh Oriental Manuscripts Library and Research Institute, Hyderabad.

Holy Quran: This copy of the gilded Quran transcribed by the famous Abbasid calligrapher Yaqut-al- Mustasimi who was the calligrapher in the court of last Abbasid Caliph. Colophon shows that, this copy of the Holy Quran was written in 1247 A.D. It is more than seven hundred years old and in a best state of preservation. This copy of the Quran has official seals of two kings, Muhammad Quli Qutb Shah and Mughal Emperor Muhmmed Shah.

Diwan-e-Ghalib: It is certified collection of almost all forms of Urdu and Persian poems by Mirza Ghalib. Contains Reekhta, Ghazalyat, Qataat, Rubaiyaat and Tarqeema. Transcribed in 1267 A.H. in good Nastaleeq in 44 pages.

Akhlaq-e-Nasiri: The manuscript is written by none other than Khwaja Nasiruddin of Tus. Written in Persian in good Nastaleeq in the year 1085 A.H.

Majmua-e-Tawarikh-e-Mehr: This manuscript contains important literary, historical and cultural information of that time apart from a short biography of the poet Wazeeruddin Muhammad Mehr which is not yet edited and published.

Kashkole: The manuscript contains unpublished verses of some of the important poets. These are Ghazals, Nauhas, Marsiyas, Salaams, Manaqib and Riwayateen.

Apart from the above mentioned manuscripts, the Library houses foolwing very important manuscripts in its possession:

- Masnawi Ghawwasi
- Guldasta
- Masnawi Behram-o-Gul-e-Andam
- Qasas-ul-Ambiya
- Khiraj Naama
- Ghalib ka Khudnawisht Khatt
- Kaleela-wa-Dimna
- Samaveda- Ramaneeya Sabha
- Samveda-Sankara Sabha
- Samveda-Tamrapanni Sabha
- Sarva Sammata Sikhsha Bhasyam-Alamuri Manchi Bhat
- Rashtra Nibhandhanam-Kavyakanta Ganpati Muni
- Amara Nighavatuvu-Krotpalli Sundararamaiah
- Bhargava Purananamu-Bahari Pomanayakudu
- Tatva Sangrah Ramayanamu-Akundi Kameshwara Kavi
- Andhra Tulasi Ramayanamu-Manda Kameshwara Kavi
- Anubhava Vaidyamu-Vankayala Narsimham

A folio from mss. Al-Quran-al-Majid, Scribed by Yaqut-al-Mustasimi, APGOMLRI, Hyderabad (courtesy: NAMAMI)

Automation

The website of the Institute contains some very valuable information about its collection and services which has been developed by National Informatics Centre. The digitized biggest manuscript of the Library and a few printed books has been accessed on its Website. The catalogue of the Library is not available on the Web.

Digitization

In this regard the Institute has signed a MoU with Noor Micro Film Center, New Delhi and Islamic Republic of Iran to complete its project of digitization of its entire collections. On 30th March, 2007 His Excellency Hussain Ravesh, Council General of the Islamic Republic of Iran in India has inaugurated the conservation and digitization of the manuscripts in the collection of the Manuscripts Library and Research Institute. This project also includes the repair, binding, fumigation and preparation of comprehensive catalogues of the entire collection. .[3]

It has digitized its 7, 698 manuscripts of 6.60 lakh pages of palm leaf and paper manuscripts from its own collection.

The MRC of National Mission for Manuscripts has been functioning in this Institute since 2005 and conducted a state wide survey in 2006. It found a total number of 2.63 lakh manuscripts in the State. A Manuscripts Week was organized from 4-9 February 2007 to bring manuscripts awareness among the people.

The Institute has digitized its biggest manuscript with help of M/S Sritree; an organisation working closely with research institutions in India. About 159 volumes of the Work have been already completed. Three printed books were also digitized and E-book generation is under process. For this purpose, a 16 member team is working on these manuscripts. Due to following qualities, the Library chosen to digitize this very important manuscript:

- Contains World's largest database of Sanskrit Words.
- Spread over 3, 80,000 pages written by a single person.
- It is the single largest manuscript in the World.
- It is the only rare manuscript written over a period of 35years.
- It is the only biggest manuscript available on the Web.

Other Activities

Apart from collectiong and preserving the rare manuscripts and printed books, the Institute is also conducting lecture series of Nipunasaravanthi on various topics related to manuscripts. It is also conducting seminars and exhibitions on manuscripts in rural and urban areas. It has also been engaged in organizing meetings on the occasions like World Heritage Day.

Today, the Library has an excellent collection of 7,876 books and 24,040 manuscripts and 716 microfilm rolls.

The following table provides us the number of printed books and manuscripts available in the Institute:

S.No.	*Language*	*Number of Printed Books*	*Number of Manuscripts*
1.	Telugu	--------	1,895
2.	Sanskirit	--------	4,311
3.	Tamil	--------	250
4.	Kannada	-------	65
5.	Hindi	------	14
6.	Marathi	-------	84
7.	English	--------	29
8.	Arabic	-------	6,337
9.	Persian	--------	8,915
10.	Urdu	---------	1,674
11.	Turkish	-------	14
12.	Punjabi	--------	04
13.	Sindhi	-------	03
14.	Pushto	-------	03
15.	Hindi in Urdu Script	--------	67
16.	Oriya	-------	359
	Total Collection	**7,876**	**24,024**

3. The Asiatic Society Library, Kolkata

Profile of the Library

The Asiatic Society, Kolkata is a premier oriental institution of the Country which was established by Sir William Jones in 1784. The library of the Asiatic Society is a grand stray, glory and honour of its parent institution. Its importance lies in its unique and rich contents of documentary resources. Most of its collections have been gifted by eminent personalities of the World. The main objective of the Society is to launch research projects on language, literature, culture and socio-economical aspect. It is the oldest repository of materials of culture, both artistic and intellectual in this Sub-continent. It has a vast collection of rare and valuable books, old manuscripts, oil paintings, coins etc. of both Hindu and Muslims periods. The Society undertakes programmes relating to development of library system, development of museum and its user facilities, augmentation of research and publication programmes. It also undertakes research projects in North-Eastern Region. During the period 2009-2010, the Asiatic Society has strengthened it research activities and the work relating to restoration of oil paintings, conservation and preservation of manuscripts and other archival documents of historical value are attended to. The review of its performance conducted by the Ministry of Culture for the last few years indicated that the Asiatic Society has been providing valuable service to the academicians, research scholars and to the general public, who are interested in the rare manuscripts, books and paintings.[4]

The collection of the Library has been categorised into following groups:

- Printed books and periodicals,
- Manuscripts and archives and
- Museum objects.

Further the Printed Books Department has following four sections viz:

- European Languages
- Sanskrit and other Modern Languages
- Perso-Arabic and Urdu and
- Sino-Tibetan and South Asian Languages.

The Library has got very good collection of books, journals and manuscripts and some of them are unique and rare material. Printed books of this Library comprises in almost all major languages of the world. There are about 1, 49,000 volumes particularly rich in works on Indology and Asiatic Lore, and in standard philological and scientific serials. The Library preserves more than 80,000 journals in many languages.[5]

The Society is a unique institution having served as fountainhead of all literary and scientific activities. It is responsible for the birth of universities, scientific surveys, museums, libraries and other cultural institutions in India. With the establishment of the library of the Society begins the history of modern libraries in India. The government has declared the Society as an institution of national importance. It is engaged in the research of remarkably varied subjects. The Society also organizes workshops and training programmes, exhibitions, seminars, lectures relating to various subjects. The library of the Asiatic Society is the oldest of its kind in modern India.

Publications

From its very inception, it has been publishing various research journals and documents on Oriental Series. Sir William Jones himself translated many masterpieces e.g. Bhagavata Gita, Sakuntala, Gita Govinda and many more.

But, perhaps one of the most renowned publications of the Society is 'Bibliotheca Indica' consisting of a series of several hundred oriental texts in Sanskrit, Arabic, Persian, Bengali, Tibetan, and other Asian Languages.

The Society regularly published Asiatic Researches, Journal of Asiatic Society, Proceedings of the Society and a very large and substantial number of scholarly oriental publications. A monthly serial under the name of 'Bibliotheca Indica' started publication from 1848.

The Society has also started compiling and publishing excellent descriptive catalogues of Sanskrit, vernacular and Arabic, Persian and Urdu manuscripts preserved under the Society's care since the last quarter of the 19th century. Separate catalogues were printed for Arabic, Persian and Urdu manuscripts. The Sanskrit catalogues included entries for Magadh, Bengali, Hindi, Kannada, Telugu, and Marathi works. A union catalogue of Sanskrit works at the Society, Sanskrit College, Calcutta and Sanskrit College, Banaras was also prepared. Mitra's first catalogue, published in 1877 was followed by a long series of catalogues of manuscripts. The catalogues published by the Society are the best specimens of descriptive cataloguing in India. The first volume in this series appeared as early as in 1895 (the volume number was changed and the contents revised later on). The Series continued till recently. The Sanskrit manuscripts have been described in 14 volumes, the latest one having been published in 1887. Scholars such as Mm. Haraprasada Sastri, Hrishikesh Sastri, Siva Chandra Guinn, Nilamani Chakravarti, Bhavabhuti Vidyaratna, Ashutosh Tarkatirtha, Nanigopal Banerji, Jogendranath Gupta, Narendra Chandra Vedantatirtha, Chintaharan Chakravarti, Satyaranjan Banerji, et al. have been the compilers and editors of different volumes. Besides, the Society has brought out quite a few volumes of catalogues of Rajasthani, Bengali, Assamese, Tibetan, Arabic, and Persian and Urdu manuscripts.[6]

The Society is supposed to do rigorous works in the direction of research and publication and the same is also directed by the Working Group on Art and Culture for XI Five-Year Plan and Proposals for XI Five-Year Plan (2007-12) & Annual Plan (2007-08) Ministry of Culture, Government of India, New Delhi, January, 2007, in following words:

> "Since, research and publication are interrelated; it should now be the policy of the Asiatic Society to undertake the publication of books of the Bibliotheca Indica series which are still deemed valuable and the publication of the research-work which may be considered meritorious by a committee of experts. With a view to remove the mismatch between resources and acceptable projects, the Society should spare no efforts toward resource conservation by re-indexing, reproducing, restoring and editing documents which are yet to be properly preserved. Resource enhancement may be achieved by the introduction of modern bibliographical service. The promotion of the sale of the Society's numerous publications through electronic publicity is a categorical imperative. The Society should take up the project of descriptive cataloguing which are yet to be completed. The extensive digitization through upgrading internal resources or through selective outsourcing is also to taken up."

Renowned Manuscripts

The Asiatic Society Library holds around 47,000 manuscripts in its collection. Manuscripts collection of the Library holds rich quality manuscripts in Indian languages and scripts e.g. Assamese, Bengali, Gujrati, Gurmukhi, Kanarese, Urdu, Marathi, Modi, Nagari, Newari, Oriya, Rajasthani, Sarada, Armenian, Sinhalese, Arabic, Persian, Pushto, Javanese, Turkish, Burmese, Chinese, Siamese, Tibetan etc. The materials used in manuscripts are also varied e.g. Palm and Palmyra leaves, Barks of different trees, and papers of various grades.[7]

The Library preserves manuscripts in twenty six scripts and languages. The Library also posses, the world famous manuscript of Shahnama by Firdausi inscribed in 15th century. There were among them many old and more works including a great number of beautifully illuminated manuscripts of the Holy Quran. An exceedingly well written old text of Gulistan, said to be the first copy from the original manuscript of the author and a codex of the Padshah Nama leaving an autograph of the emperor Shah Jahan, were among them. On the abolition of the Fort William College, the whole of its Arabic, Persian, Urdu and Sanskrit works, mostly in manuscript form, collected at great expense and trouble, were place in the custody of the Asiatic Society.

Apart from above mentioned well-known manuscript, the Library houses following very important and rare manuscripts in its collection:

Maiteryavyakarana : Maiteryavyakarana is the 'prophetic story of the future Buddha' as Maitreya is the 'future Buddha' or 'Buddha to come' and Vyakarana in Buddhist Sanskirit means 'prophecy' or prediction regarding the future Buddhas. The text was written in the period of Buddhist literature which forms a transition from the Sthaviravada to Mahayana Buddhist schools. As a text, it is a source of ecclesiastic and iconographic inspiration to people of Buddhist countries and was very popular throughout the Buddhist World.

This manuscript was written in the fifty seventh year of Gopaladeva of the Pala dynasty of Bengal, i.e. probably in the fifty seventh year of Gopala II, who ascended the throne in about 940 A.D. The text is composed in prose form in Sanskirit in a combination of both Kutila and Ranjan scripts. This is one of the rarest compositions among the Buddhist texts. The manuscript is on seven folios of palm leaf.

Samputatika : This manuscript is extremely unique, as it is manual on rituals in Buddhist tantric traditions, and the mystic philosophy of the macro and micro cosmos. It is written on palm leaf with ink in Sanskirit and the script is in old Newari and Gaudi. The micro cosmos is a minute representation of the macro cosmos, in the Universe. Buddhist tantra philosophy seeks to bring the micro cosmos in harmony with the macro cosmos which is the ultimate liberation. The manuscript is unique because of its early date.

Kalachakravatara : It was authored by Abhayakara Gupta, a prolific writer of Tantaric Dogmatics, Liturgy and Mandala, and an abbot of Vikramshila Monastery during the reign of the Pala king Rampala. The text reflects on both

Tantra as well as early Budhist mysticism including the philosophy of the Universe and the mystical philosophy of Cosmology.

The manuscript dates back to Saka 1047/1125 A.D., so it was possibly written during Abhayakara Gupta's lifetime. It is palm leaf manuscript written in Sanskirit and scribed by Dhanashri Mitra.

Kubjikamata : The Kubjikamata is an ancient text dating to about the 3rd Century A.D. A scripture of Kaula sect, Vamachara Tantrics, and this text was extremely important in the development of Tantric Practices and Philosophy. It traces the development of the Cult of of the virgin goddess Kubjika. It prescribes different methods of virgin worship.

This manuscript is very old, dating to the 7th Century, written in the later Gupta period. As, this text is considered to be revealed, no author can be scribed. The scribe is also unknown. The language of this palm leaf manuscript is Sanskirit and the script is version of Brahmi that dates to the later Gupta period.

Apart from the above mentioned manuscripts, the Library also possess following very important manuscripts in its collection:

- Brihati
- Amrita Vindu
- Gulistan
- Padshah Namah
- Dasveliyan
- Jaya Purana by Shri Pada Nandhi
- Bal Bharat by Shri Madan Chand
- Pur Vachan Saar by Hem Raj.

Apart from having a great number of invaluable printed books and manuscripts, the Society also preserves inscriptions and coins which are closely related to books. They differ only in material in which they are preserved but are fully as valuable as written history, and at times much more so, being far more authentic. Their acquisition and development has engaged the attention of the Society from the very establishment, and some of the most brilliant discoveries in

Indian history have been thereby made. A large number of these inscriptions and coins were transferred to Indian Museum at a later date.

Roman, Greek, Bactrian, Indo-Scythian, Sassanian and Gupta coins were acquired for the Society. Later, Norwegian, Delhi-Pathans, Bengal-Pathans, Hindu and Buddhist coins were gradually added to the collection.

A folio from mss. Maiteryavyakarana, ASL, Kolkata (courtesy: NAMAMI)

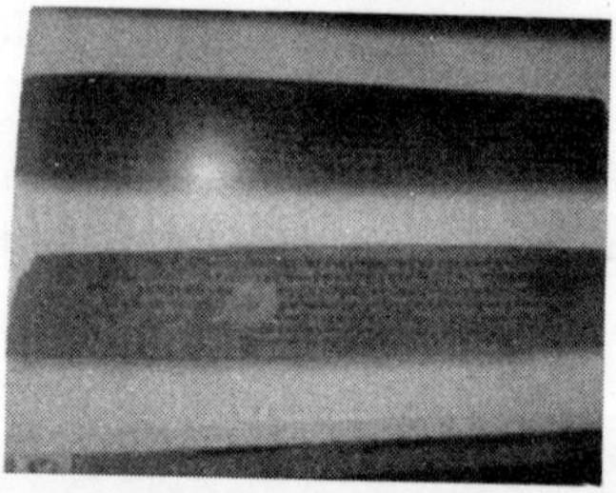

A folio of mss. Kubjikamata, ASL, Kolkata(courtesy: NAMAMI)

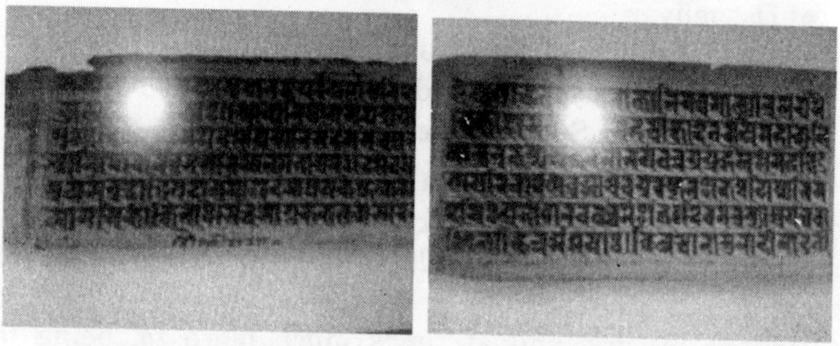

Two folios of mss. Maitreyvyakarana, ASL, Kolkata(courtesy: NAMAMI)

Automation

The library of the Asiatic Society is still in its infancy as far as computerization or automation is concerned. Though, the books of the Institution has not only arranged properly but also has been utilized by many scholars. There is urgent need to do modernization work in this direction. The website of the Society provided detailed description of its books and valuable manuscripts.

Digitization

The library of the Asiatic Society at Kolkata is still infancy as far as digitization of rare documents and manuscripts are concerned. It has a wide range of valuable manuscripts, important paper documents and printed volumes in its Library. Therefore, it is necessary to digitize its collection as early as possible. The Library needs to start the digitization work with collaboration of government organisation for better access to its valuable collections.

Other Activities

The Asiatic Society has a well established museum which preserves large collection of paintings, manuscripts, sculptures, bronze coins and inscriptions.[8]

The Society has also organizes seminars, symposia and conferences on various subjects from time to time. The Society also encourages rigorous research activities in numerous fields of interest.

Total collection of printed books and manuscripts in its Library is approximately 1, 49,000 and 47,000 respectively. Language wise data about its printed books and manuscripts collection is not available.

Asiatic Society of Mumbai , Mumbai

4. Asiatic Society of Mumbai, Mumbai

Profile of the Library

The Asiatic Society of Mumbai, a learned society in the field of Asian studies, is based in Mumbai, India. It can trace its origin to the Literary Society of Bombay which first met in Mumbai on November 26, 1804, and was founded by Sir James Mackintosh. The Society was established in 1804, as a branch of the Royal Asiatic Society in London.

It was formed with the intention of 'promoting useful knowledge, particularly such as is now immediately connected with India'. After the Royal Asiatic Society of Great Britain and Ireland was established in London in 1823, the Literary Society of Bombay became affiliated with it and was known as the Bombay Branch of the Royal Asiatic Society (BBRAS) since 1830. The Bombay Geographical Society merged with it in 1873, followed by the Anthropological Society of Bombay in 1896. In 1954, it was separated from the Royal Asiatic Society and renamed the Asiatic Society of Bombay. In the year 2002, it acquired its present name. It is funded by an annual grant from the central government of India.[9]

The library of the Society has over a hundred thousand books out of which 15,000 are classified as rare and valuable.

Publications

Initially, the Literary Society of Bombay published its transactions under the title, Transactions of the Literary Society of Bombay. In 1841, the Asiatic Society of Bombay commenced publishing its journal titled, Journal of the Bombay Branch of the R.A.S. From 1955 to 2002, it published its journal under the name; Journal of the Asiatic Society of Bombay and from 2002, its journal has been published under the name, Journal of the Asiatic Society of Mumbai.[10]

The Society publishes scholarly monographs which pertain to ancient Hindu, Jain and Buddhist texts. The Institute has consistently brought out its journal, albeit under different nomenclatures, which is presently known as the "Journal of the Asiatic Society of Mumbai". This erudite journal contains articles and books reviews ranging from ancient Vedic texts, Archaeology, Philology and Art. A few important publications of the Society are as follows:

- Buddhaghosa by Dr. B.C. Law
- Jain Canonical Sutras by Dr. B.C. Law
- An Illustrated Aranyaka Parvan in The Asiatic Society of Bombay by Shri Karl Khandalavala and Dr. Moti Chandra
- Kavindra Kalpadruma of Kavindracharya Sarasvati edited by Prof. R.B. Athavale
- James Darmesteter remembered edited by Prof. G Lazard and Dr. D.R. Sardesai

- On the Meaning of Mahabharata by V.S. Sukhathankar
- A Descriptive Catalogue of Sanskrit and Prakrit Manuscripts, Compiled by H.D. Velankar.

Renowned Manuscripts

The Asiatic Society of Mumbai is perhaps the most legendary and talked-about in regard of its indeed invaluable collection of manuscripts, artefacts, relics, gold coins and maps and rarest of the rare books from ancient, prehistoric to historical India and the World. The Society's holdings comprise over 3,000 manuscripts in Sanskrit, Arabic, Persian, Urdu and Prakrit from all over India and Nepal. They are predominantly done on paper, but some are on palm leaf. They incorporate technical literature on Linguistics, Medicine, Astronomy, Jain and other Brahmanical literature in Sanskrit, an appendix on Buddhist manuscripts, Jain literature and manuscripts in Gujarati, Hindi and Marathi.

The rarest among the rare manuscripts collections of the Society include:

Divine Comedy: The manuscript is one of the most precious possessions of the Library written in 1350 A.D. by Dante. It is quanerrian of great beauty and excellence. The calligraphy is large, clear and attractive. The inside of the leather binding has an inscription in Italian which says: 'Magnificient book in parchament of the Divinia Commedia of Dante Aleghieri, which equals in preservation and beauty those existing in the leading libraries of Europe, especially those in the Ambrosion Library of Milan, Italy, with which it has been compared.

Shahnama of Firdausi: Another gem in the collection of the Library is an illustrated manuscript of the Shahnama. The Shahnama is an epic text that narrates the history of of the early kings of Persia (Iran) and historical episodes such as those that occurred during the reign of Yazdagir in the early 11th century A.D. and with which epic ends. The manuscript is profusely illustrated with every chapter beginning with a painting. The colophon of the manuscript mentions that it was prepared in 900 A.H. / 1495 A.D. in the city of Shiraz in Iran, a famous school of painting at the time. Moreover, the Library is also having a later version of Shahnama written in 1843 A.D.

Aranyaka Parva: This is an illustrated manuscript. The colophon folios date the manuscript to Samvat 1573/ 1516 A.D. This manuscript was copied at Yoginipura, under the rule of Sikander Lodi, for Bhanudas Chaudhari. Almost all the folios of the manuscript are commented with beautiful pictures indicative of the story described in them. The 'Aranyaka Parva' of the Mahabharata deals with the events during the 12 years of exile of the Pandavas after Yudhistira's loss at the game of dice. This manuscript comes under the collection of this Library through Dr. Bhau Daji Lad collection in 1882 along with number of other manuscripts.

Astasahasrika Prajnaparamita: Another highlight in the library's collection is the set of six palm-leaf illustrated folios from the Budhist manuscript 'Astasahasrika Prajnaparamita'of Circa 1200 A.D. Illustrated palm-leaf manuscripts painted during the reign of the Pala kings in the Bihar and Bengal were very popular at one time. They usually contain illustrations of Tantric Budhist dieties. But, the invasion by Bakhtiyar Khalji in 1200 A.D. brought about a decline in the practice of this Art in eastern India and it found a new home in the regions now known as Nepal and Tibet.

A few other renowned manuscripts in Society possession's are as follows:

- Vasupujyacharita written in 1242 A.D.
- Gautam Pricchasutra (Prakrit) written in 1350 A.D.
- Ganaratnamahodadhi of Vardhaman written in Sanskrit in 1423 A.D.
- Kalpasutra of Bhadrabahu written in Sanskrit in 15th century A.D.

- Mahabharata translated by Faizi in Persian in 18th Century.
- Risalah at-Tarjamat-az-Zahira-li-Firqa-ti-Bohrat-al-Bhahira written in17th Century.
- Sadavasyaka Sutra with Balavabodha written in old Gujarati in 1393 A.D.
- Suryasiddhanta with bhashya of Candelvara on Astronomy written in 12th Century A.D.
- Five Buddhist caskets excavated in the ancient port town Sopara near the suburb of Nala Sopara.
- Nal-u-Daman by Maulvi Faizi Fayyazi.
- Aina-i-Akbari by Abul Fazal Faizi bin Mubarak.
- Nasab Namah by Wajh-ud-Din.
- Mirat-i-Sikandari by Sikander bin Muhammad Manjhu.
- Padshah Naama by Muhammad Waris.
- Tarikh-i-Gujarat by Ranchorjee Amarjee Diwan.
- Disatir by Mulla Firoz.
- Al-Jawahar-fi-Jamil min-al-Sirat by Muhhar bin Muhammad bin Nadir.
- Qissa-i-Rustam Ali.
- Naqliyyat-i-Hindi.

Automation

The Asiatic Society of Mumbai has developed an impressive website which contains valuable information about its origin, aims, publications, library and other similar academic activities. The Online Public Access Catalogue (OPAC) of printed books is uploaded on its website. Though, information about printed collections and rare manuscripts of its Library has not been provided in Society's website.

Digitization

Back issues of the ASM Journal (1841 – 2007) have been digitized by M/s. Puja Soft Technologies Pvt. Ltd. The unique and notable items in these CDs is the comprehensive text search facility now made available for the first time to researchers, scholars, general readers and the students interested in ASJs which were edited by legendaries like Dr. P.V. Kane. A researcher can look for any word/term/ text, etc. using any Desktop search tool or even Windows Search facility. This work will save a lot of time which was otherwise required for searching topics in these journals.

Other Activities

The numismatic collection of 11,829 coins includes a gold coin of Kumaragupta I, a rare gold Mohur (Inscription) of Mughal king Akbar and coins issued by Shivaji. Its map collection comprises 1, 300 maps.[11]

The Society has been actively providing a forum for cultural and public events, organizing and conducting a host of lectures, book readings and film screenings. In order to inculcate a sense of community ownership and pride, the Society organizes heritage walks and commemoration lectures on eminent personalities. It has instituted several endowments, awards and research fellowships which are directed toward enhancing knowledge bases.[12]

Bhandarkar Oriental Research Institute, Pune

6. Bhandarkar Oriental Research Institute, Pune

Profile of the Library

The Bhandarkar Oriental Research Institute, Pune, was founded on July 6, 1917 to commemorate the name and the work of Ramakrishna Gopal Bhandarkar, the foremost pioneer of scientific orientology in India.The Institute is a public organization registered under Act XXI 1860 (a public trust). It is partially supported by annual earmarked grants from the Maharashtra government. The Institute has one of the largest collections of rare books and manuscripts spanning over 1,25,000 books and over 29,510 manuscripts collected over a period of ninety years covering practically every aspect of orientology. This collection covers several languages and scripts such as Sanskrit, Prakrit, Indian regional languages, and classical, Asian and European languages. The BORI Library, recently named after the legendary Dr. R. N. Dandekar, is internationally recognized as a specialized library in the field of orientology.

The library of the Institute is a matter of its legimate conceit, both for the rare and rich collection and for its continual use by scholars from all over the world. The Library is fortunate in having been presented to it the Siamese, Chinese, Japanese, Korean and Burmese, volumes of Tripitaka. It is a home to above 1,25,000 handpicked books pertaining to all aspects of the Oriental Studies. About 20,000 of the books are quite rare to find the world over. Books in over twenty five (25) Indian and European languages are housed here. The chronological range of the books spans over the early days of printing till date are available for the benefit of scholars.

The Library was founded with a valuable personal collection of about 2, 200 books donated by Sir Ramakrishna Gopal Bhandarkar himself. Stalwarts like P. K. Gode, A. D. Pusalkar, S. V. Sohoni, R. N. Dandekar, P. V. Bapat and P. L. Vaidya have donated their personal collections to the Library. Volumes of esteemed national and international journals are procured in exchange with the Annals.[13]

Publications

The Institute publishes its annual journal 'Annals of the Bhandarkar Oriental Research Institute'. The most prominent publications of the Institute are:

1. Critical edition of the Mahabharata (19 Volumes)
2. Critical edition of the Harivamsha (3 Volumes)
3. Pratika Index (2 Volumes)
4. Critically constituted text of Mahabharata and Harivamsha
5. Mahabharata : Cultural Index (2 Volumes)
6. The Vedic Bibliography edited by Dr. R. N. Dandekar
7. Descriptive Catalogues of manuscripts in the Govt. manuscripts library of the BORI
8. The Critical and Comprehensive Dictionary of the Prakrit Languages on Historical Principles (3 Volumes)
9. The Collected Works of R. G. Bhandarkar (4 Vol.)
10. History of Dharmashastra by P. V. Kane (5 Vol; 6,884 pages)
11. The Vyakaranamahabhashya of Patanjali edited by Kielhorn
12. The Paribhashendushekhara of Nagojibhatta edited by Kielhorn

13. Shribhashya of Ramanuja edited by Vasudevshastri Abhyankar
14. Sarvadarshanasamgraha of Sayana Madhava edited by Vasudevshastri Abhyankar
15. Prakrit Grammar of Hemachandra edited by P. L. Vaidya
16. Tarikh-i-Sind edited by U. M. Daudpota
17. The Paribhashasamgraha by K. V. Abhyankar
18. Devanagari editions of the Dhammasangani and the Atthasalini by P. V. Bapat and R. D. Wadekar
19. Jinaratnakosha edited by H. D. Velankar
20. Shan Chien-Pi Po-sha by P. V. Bapat and A. Hirakawa

Renowned Manuscripts

The 'one of its kind' manuscript collection at the BORI is the perfect testimony to the literary heritage living in the manuscripts. The largest part of the collection (17,877 manuscripts) is known by the name 'The Government Manuscript Library'. There are some more collections (11,633 manuscripts), too. The total number of manuscripts amounts to 29510, and still counting......the Institute maintains a few important collection of manuscripts in its Library such as :

Kashmir Manuscripts: This collection (1875 - 76) comprises Birch Bark Manuscripts written in Sharada script and related related with Kashmir Shaivism, Jainism and the history of Kashmir.

Vishrambaghwada Collection of Manuscripts : Believed to have belonged to the Peshwas and the Poona Sanskrit College, Vishrambaghwada (estd. 1821)

Persian Manuscripts: Contains many illustrated and illuminated manuscripts.

Jaina Manuscripts: A few thousand manuscripts related with Jaina literature and philosophy.

The Collection of Rigveda Manuscripts: Recognized as a vital part of the Memory of the World Heritage Collection by the UNESCO.

A few very important and rare manuscripts in BORI's possession are:

Rigveda Samhita: The Rigveda is one of the four main Vedas or texts that form the basis of the Hindu faith. Considered to be the oldest literary document in the World, it was composed in the form of poems, songs and prayers in praise of nature's bounty. This valuable treasure of the ancient world was composed perhaps 3000 years ago and was orally transmitted for generations before finally coming down to us in manuscript form. One of the reasons this text is considered to be important because it captures the imagination, aspiration, ambition, and ideology of people who lived more than three millennia ago.

This manuscript of the Rigveda Samhita is extremely rare as it written on birch bark, a support material used exclusively in Kashmir. It dates to 51 Kashmir Era. The text is composed in Sanskirit in Sharada script. The famous german Indologist, F. Max Muller, used this particular manuscript for his critical edition of the Rigveda, complete with a translation of its famous commentary by Sayana in 1849 A.D. The scribe of this manuscript was Bhatta Bhimaswami. It was procured by George Buhler, Professor of Sanskirit at Elphinstone College, Mumbai during his third trip to Kashmir, in one of the efforts in surveying indian manuscripts.

Bhagavata Purana: The Bhagavata Purana is one of the most important texts of Hindu mythology and said to have been composed by Vyasa. Historically, this text is important from the point of view of Bhakti Movement as it focuses on Bhakti Yoga or 'loving devotion to the supreme God' in which Vishnu is seen as god of all gods.

The manuscript at BORI, written by Jasvant Bhattaraka in 1648A.D. is considered exceptional not only because it has 128 beautiful coloured paintings in the Rajput style, but also because it was entirely illustrated by a painter Shahbuddin, a Muslim. The margins of the text are well defined and those of the illustrations are marked with red and yellow pigment. This manuscript was acquired for the BORI collection by Prof. Ghate from Udaipur. The text is written in Sanskirit language making use of Devanagari script on folios of hand made paper.

Cikitsasarasangraha: The Cikitsasarasangraha was originally composed in the 12th century by Vangadatta. This manuscript on the medical treatise was written shortly thereafter by the scribe Jalasuta Ranasimha of Bijapur in 1320A.D. It is one of the largest compilations on medical knowledge that draws heavily from older works related to medicine. It also contains copious extracts from the work of the 8th century physician Madhava who wrote about diseases, their causes, symptoms and compilations with a special focus on small pox. This manuscript is also one of the earliest known manuscripts on paper as paper is said to have arrived in India in the 12th century i.e. around the time that the author of this text lived.

The Cikitsasarasangraha is certainly the oldest paper manuscript in the collection at the Bhandarkar Oriental Research Institute. Since, it was acquired during the 1880s; two printed editions of the texts have been published. The manuscript is composed in Sanskirit in Devanagari script with prishthimitras.

Mahabhashya: The Mahabhashya was written in 1490 A.D., although the date of the original composition of this linguistic treatise in Sanskirit remains unknown. It is believed that a large part of it was authored by the famous linguist Patanjali. A monumental work, it is essentially a commentary on the more technical aspects of Panini's grammer and Katyayana's critical annotations of Panini's Sutras. Written in conversational style, it is one of the three knowen works of Patanjali.

It was acquired for BORI by Prof. Kielhorn during his treks across Bombay Presidency in search of Sanskirit manuscripts in early 1880s. Subsequently, he also published a crtical edition of Mahabhashya in three volumes under the Bombay Sanskirit Series. Jogeshwer, the scribe, has composed this manuscript in very fine calligraphy in small yet clearly discernible Devanagari characters with pristhamatras on hand made paper.

Upamitibhavaprapanchakatha: The Upamitibhavaprap -anchakatha was composed in and written at around the same time (i.e. 906A.D.), making it one of the oldest palm leaf texts in the country and certainly the oldest in the BORI collection. Acquired by Prof. Keilhorn in the year 1880-81, the text is important in the context of Jain literature-being a narrative text of the Shvetambara Sect of the Jainism, one of the two major sects of Jainism. The Shvetambara Sect broke away about 200 years after Mahavira and has a large following today. A few of the words that occur in this work are also found in Nalshadhacharita, an epic poem about the love between king Nala and the princess Damayanti. In Sanskirit language with a script that is painted in Devanagari characters with pristhamatras, Upamitibhavaprapanchakatha was critically edited in the years 1899-1914 by P. Peterson and H. Jacobi, and subsequently translated into German and Gujarati.

Shahnama of Firdausi: An illustrated manuscript produced 900 years back, written by none other than legendary scholar of Persian language Firdausi.

Sivalilamrta: It is an old illustrated manuscript.

These and such other manuscripts, as well as an Astrolabe, have been kept as exhibits in the Library.

When the Bhandarkar Oriental Research Institute was founded in 1917, the then Government of Bombay handed over its entire collection of manuscripts. The same collection is known as Government Manuscripts Collection. The Institute has, all these years, been looking after the preservation, lending out, and cataloguing of these manuscripts, and, as the government reports would testify, the work of the Institute in this connection has been most exemplary.

The Bhandarkar Oriental Research Institute (BORI) has been working with the National Mission for Manuscripts as MCC since September, 2003. It has so far taken preventive care of 1,217 manuscripts and given curative conservation treatment to 29 manuscripts. Microfilming of about over a million folios (including those of about 4,000 un-catalogued manuscripts) was carried out at the Institute, under the auspices of the Indira Gandhi National Centre for Arts, New Delhi, and completed recently.

Three folios of mss. Bhagavata Purana, BORI, Pune (courtesy: NAMAMI)

Two folios of mss. Cikitsasarasangraha, BORI, Pune (courtesy: NAMAMI)

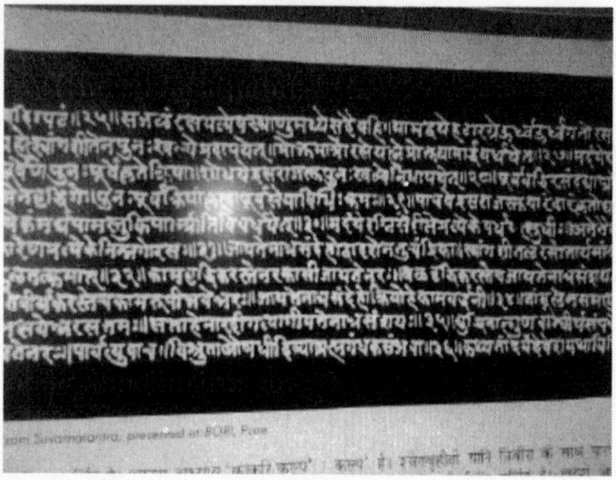

A folio of mss. Suvarnatantra, BORI, Pune (courtesy:NAMAMI)

Automation: The library of Institute has started the computerization/ automation work, but it is still in infancy. There is an urgent need to add more computer systems in this great Institution to accelerate the computerization work on its printed volumes and rare valuable manuscripts. The Library has a vision to develop a modern and up-to-date information and documentation work, so as, it will survive in the era of Information Technology.

Digitization: The Institute, with its solid foundation in magnanimous contributions to oriental research and with the help of its scholarly infrastructure of the present day, aspires for goals still higher!

The steps thereto run through the following:

- Development of Digital Library for Bhandarkar Oriental Research Institute (BORI)
- Preservation and protection of the content of rare books and manuscripts and archives of the Mahabharata and Prakrit Dictionary
- World wide access on Internet
- National and international collaborative oriental research
- State-of-the-art Computer and Networking infrastructure for creating and accessing the Digital Library.

- Automation of library management system
- Creation of on-line catalogue of books and manuscripts for web access.
- Digitization of rare books and manuscripts
- Digital database of the cultural index of the critical edition of Mahabharata.

Digital database of the comprehensive and critical Prakrit Dictionary. Virtual Museum of manuscripts, Photographs and Artifacts

- Development of computation research tools such as Advanced Multilingual Search, Study of occurrences, Sanskrit and Prakrit dictionaries, ontological research, etc.
- Interactive Digital Portal for content, communications, collaboration and commerce

The National Mission for Manuscripts has recognized the service of BORI by declaring BORI a Manuscript Resource Centre (MRC) and the sole Manuscript Conservation Centre (MCC) in Maharashtra state. The Manuscript Resource Centre at Bhandarkar Oriental Research Institute has been functioning since September 2003. The MRC has so far documented **55,500** manuscripts and prepared electronic data of 46, 308 manuscripts for the Manus Granthavali. The survey conducted by more than 30 members has covered 101 collections in Maharashtra, covering 17 districts during the survey. The information pertains mostly to Sanskrit manuscripts, with some Marathi manuscripts as well. The MRC has also covered 123 institutions and 30 individual collections through with assistance from its scholars.[14]

Other Activities: The Institute organizes learned lectures by guest scholars under its various memorial lectureships. The All India Oriental Conference, various seminars and scholarly discussions are also organized by the Institute.

The Library holds approximately 1, 25,000 printed books and 29,510 manuscripts in various Indian languages. The data about language wise break-up of the printed books and manuscripts of the Library is not available.

Central Institute of Budhist Studies, Leh

7. Central Institute of Buddhist Studies(CIBS), Leh

Profile of the Library: Formerly known as the School of Buddhist Philosophy, the Central Institute of Buddhist Studies was established in 1959 to develop a comprehensive knowledge of Buddhism, which includes the study of Ancient Shastras, Culture, Philosophy and History, and languages such as Hindi, Sanskrit, English, Tibetan (Bhoti) and Pali. The Institute was also set up to translate Buddhist manuscripts into Sanskrit, Hindi, English and other Indian languages, to collect, preserve and publish rare manuscripts and to facilitate research on Buddhism. It has worked as a nodal resource centre for Buddhism in the local area for several years. It was established with the aim of satisfying the inquisitive needs of the local people regarding Buddhism and Buddhist studies. The Central Institute of Buddhist Studies has applied for the status of a deemed university, and its status is under revision.

The main aim of the Central Institute of Buddhist Studies lies in developing the personality of the students by instilling the values of Buddhist philosophy, literature and arts into their thought process. For achieving the aim few methods have been designed, such as:

- Study of Buddhism in all its totality, including its history, philosophy and ancient shastras.
- Study of languages connected with Buddhism, such as Pali, Bhoti (Tibetan), Sanskrit and English.
- Study of subjects like general science, social studies and comparative philosophy, history, political science, arithmetic, economics.
- Translation of Buddhist manuscripts into Indian languages like Hindi, Sanskrit and into English.
- Collecting, preserving and publishing rare manuscripts.
- Researching on topics related to Buddhism
- Collecting and preserving historical artifacts.
- Study of Amchi (Bodhi Medical Science), Thankas (Buddhist Paintings), Scripts, religious carvings on wood, and other sculptures related to Buddhism.
- Arranging seminars on Buddhism and organizing exhibitions of Buddhist artifacts for popularizing Buddhism.
- Conducting mass literacy programs.

The library of the Institute has a fine collection of over 20,000 manuscripts, books, reports and journals associated to Buddhist Studies. The Reference Section of the Library has a range of tools such as Encyclopedia Britannica, Encyclopedia of Religion and Ethics, Encyclopedia of Buddhism etc. The Library also subscribes to a few major Indological Series of Oriental Research Institutes such as Pali Text Society, Buddhist Sanskrit Text Series of Darbhanga etc. In addition, the Library has collected major original and collected works on Buddhism of momentous researchers from all over the world, besides subscribing to 30 to 40 research journals.

For modernizing the infrastructure and other facilities, the Institute has completed the construction of Academic Block, Library Building, Administrative Block, forty (40) staff quarters of type three , two (02) hostel blocks for hundred (100) students each, sports stadium, internal and approach road, part of the water distribution system, pump and generator house and commissioned during the 10th Five Year Plan by incurring an expenditure of Rs.1, 548.40 lakhs including the anticipated expenditure for the current financial year.[15]

Publications

To achieve its aims and objectives, the Institute is translating the Bhoti/Tibetan rare books into Hindi and published them. The Institute is also bringing out a number of publications mainly under two series namely 'Baudha-Himalaya Granthamala Series' and 'Ladakha-Prabha Series'. The Institute also publishes the valuable manuscripts that are worthwhile for publication. The scholars presented papers in the seminars are also published in the form of books titled 'Ladakha-Prabha Series'. Ten volumes have been so far brought out by the Institute. Besides, a proposal has already been approved by the Board to publish a 'Research Journal' of the Institute. For all these purposes, an amount of Rs. 25.00 lakhs has been proposed during the eleventh Five Year Plan. The Institute has published one Tibetan-Hindi Dictionary completed by Rev.Lobzang Jampal.[16]

Renowned Manuscripts

The library of the Institute houses a brilliant collection of Buddhist manuscripts since its very inception. It preserves over 10,000 manuscripts specially dealing with Buddhism besides other subjects.

Automation

The Institute has developed an impressive website of its own recently in 2011 with almost all valuable information about it.

Since, the Information Technology is very essential component in modernization of any kind of organizations and the government of India is also desires to provide every type of assistance in modernizing it. Therefore, to provide better facilities to the students of the Institute, a proposal is under process to computerize not only its Administration Section but also its library very soon. For the above mentioned work, an amount of Rs. 25.00 lakhs has been sanctioned under the Eleventh Five Year Plan.[17]

Digitization

During the ninth five year plan, the Institute has received support from the government for improvement of infrastructure and digitalization. The MRC at the Central Institute of Buddhist Studies, Leh has been working with the Mission since October 2003. It has primarily focused on the survey and documentation of Buddhist (mostly Tibetan) collections of manuscripts in the area. The MRC has done active work in the difficult terrains of Ladakh, dotted with Buddhist monasteries, which are the storehouses of manuscripts. With the team of three scholars and three officials, the MRC has documented and prepared **6,958** electronic data of Tibetan, Bhoti and Buddhist manuscripts in **755** collections in and around Leh, Zanskar and Nubrary Valley. The MRC has conducted 50 publicity programmes in various monasteries, which received phenomenal response of the people of this region.

To conserve these manuscripts a Manuscript Conservation Centre (MCC) was established at CIBS. A conservation laboratory with basic infrastructure and equipment was set up by the central team for conservation at the Mission which visited CIBS. More than 3,592 folios have undergone preventive conservation along with curative conservation of 3,000 manuscripts.[18]

Other Activities

The Institute is running 29 feeder schools known as Gonpa/ Nunnery School in different monasteries of Ladakh to provide the basic elementary education to the young monks in addition to monastic education and the present strength of students of these schools is 731. The Institute has also a branch school at

Zanskar in Kargil district with the strength of 173 students from Class I to VIII.

The Institute offers fellowships for research work leading to award of doctorates in the field of Buddhism. At present, three research scholars are pursuing research for Ph.D.

Besides, the Institute has built up a modest Archaeological Museum with good collection of antiquities and other objects. The collection includes Sculpture and Thanka paintings of Ladakh and antique photographs and replicas from many historical places of India.

During the year under report the Institute published one book titled Ladakh Prabha VIII & IX, the collected articles/ papers of the All India. The Institute has been organizing national/international seminars/symposium on the subject relating to the aims and objectives of the Institute to provide the benefit to the staff, students as well as to other seekers of the knowledge. The Institute organized an international seminar in August, 2004 on the subject "Buddhism for Twenty First Century: An International Prospective". Scholars from all over the world gathered and the seminar was a grand success. Besides, the Institute frequently arranges lecture series on various subjects relevant to Buddhist Philosophy and Buddhist Studies by inviting eminent scholars from other universities and institutions for a specific period in a session. To meet the expenses on this account a sum of Rs.50.00 lakhs has been proposed during the Eleventh Five Year Plan.[19]

The Library of the Institute is one of the best libraries in the entire Buddhist Himalayan region with the collection of 21,091books in different languages.

Connemara Public Library, Chennai

8. Connemara Public Library, Chennai

Profile of the Library

The origin of this Library goes back to later part of 19th century. The, then British rulers recognized the importance of the library service and decided to establish for the first time a public library in Madras Presidency during the last century by an enlightened administrator Lord Connemara, the then Governor of Madras during 1886-1891. The foundation stone of the Library lay on 22nd March 1890. It is a world class library with teak shelves and standard glass windows with a very tall ceiling reflecting colonial ambience was the idea of the H. Irvin, the consulting architect of Madras Presidency. Continuously growing, the Library had significant additions, the most important being a grand three storey building added in 1974. In the year 1999; the Library has added one more three storey building to accommodate its large collections. The new building, which was added to the Library in 1974, has a vast collection of books, a much sought after text-book section, a periodicals hall, a video room, an entire floor for books from the Indian languages, a Braille Library and an IAS Study Centre. Over six lakhs (6, 00,000) books are available in the Library. The Connemara is a place where gems can be found at every corner, but only by the discerning eye.

It is one of the national public depositaries libraries subsequent to the National Library, Kolkata, Delhi Public

Library, Delhi and Asiatic Society Library, Mumbai which receive a copy of all books, newspapers and periodicals published in India. Apart from this, a good number of collections, publications and periodicals of UN and its specialized organs and Asian Development Bank were also received. Further, with the generous support of the state government, the Library receives a good number of documents every year. Founded in 1890, the Library is a repository of centuries-old publications, wherein lie some of the most respected works and collections in the country. It also serves as depository library for the United Nations.[20]

The Library possesses a collection of more than 6.36 lakhs books, 2 lakhs bound volumes of periodicals, 500 maps, posters and prints, 300 video and audio tapes, discs etc, 150 sound recordings, magnetic tapes, 600 microfilms. It has been receiving more than 3,693 journals and serials and 250 newspapers.

Publications

The first printed author catalogue was brought out in 1908. In 1931, two volumes of author catalogue were printed. The supplement came in 1935 in two volumes. Likewise the periodical catalogue was printed in 1935.

The Library regularly brings out a monthly fascicule of Tamil Nadu State Bibliography since 1964 for proper coordination of classification, book selection and reference service.[21]

The Library has published two very important documents on its collections e.g.

Publication of Tamil Nadu State Bibliography of Children's Literature in 1963 and Publication of Tamil Nadu State Bibliography of Tamil Books in 1964

Renowned Manuscripts

The Library preserves some of the very rare and world famous manuscripts in its collection. Most of the manuscripts date back to 19th century and written in Tamil, Telugu, Malayalam, and Kannada languages. These manuscripts have already been microfilmed.

Some of the oldest and rarest books available in the Library are as follows:

The Bible: The Library holds an old copy of 'The Bible' written in 1608.

Memoir: It contains an account of the trade in India by Charles Lockyer written in 1711

Flora Indica: The above mentioned rare volume is written by Nicolai Laverrntii Burmanii in the year 1768.

A voyage to Suratt: A voyage to Suratt is written by J. Owington written in 1696.

Hourtus Indicus Malabaricus: It is available in 12 volumes and written by Rheed and few others during the years between 1678-1703.

Malabarians: It is an account of religion and government, learning and economy etc. inhabitants of the Malabarians published in 1717.

Memoirs: It is a memoir written by Zahir-ud-din Mohammad Babur.

Automation:

The initial computerization in this great Library has been traced in the last decade of 20th century. In April 2003, the budget increased to 20 lakhs and with the help of this increased budget, the organization has purchased more computer systems. Until 2007-08, the Library was functioning with 40 computer systems providing OPAC service, CD Rom Service, Reprography Service etc. to its clientele. The Circulation System is also computerized. The next important event in its history was to introduce Online Public Access Catalogue (OPAC) in June 2003. A touch screen system for library was another feature in its activities.[22]

Digitization

Computer Unit was installed in the Library in the year 1991. The Library has purchased many computers which were especially meant for computerization in 1998. In the next year, the Internet service was launched in the Library. The Library has started automation in the year 2000 as well as it has established a Microfilm Unit in the same year. The Web based Online Public Access Catalogue (OPAC) was implemented and member bar code introduced in 2003. Now, the catalogue is accessible through Intranet and Internet both. Internet Browsing Centre was functional from the year 2005. The Library has initiating digitization efforts with the help of government organizations.

Other activities:

From time to time, the Library has also engaged other academic activities like seminars, symposia and workshops. In the year 1966, the Library has established an Institute of Library Science. The Xerox facility as well as separate CD ROM section was established respectively in the year 1985 and 2005. A Braille Library and an IAS Study Centre was also established in the Library. The expenditure for maintaining the Library is met by the government of Tamil Nadu. However, the government of India meets fifty per cent of the recurring expenditure and two third of non-recurring expenditure in respect of maintaining the Delivery of Books Acts Section of the Library.

The total collection of printed books in the Library is 6, 36,000. The data about the collection of manuscripts is not available either in its website or elsewhere. The language wise break up of its documents is also not available.

Darul Musannefin Shibli Academy, Azamgarh

9. Darul Musannefin Shibli Academey, Azamgarh

Profile of the Library

The Darul Musannefin Shibli Academy was established on November 21, 1914, three days after the death of its founder, Maulana Shibli Nomani. He was an erudite scholar and a versatile writer. He was quick to grasp the need for a modern institution for the study of and research in the various branches of Islamic learning and oriental languages. Both logic and history seemed to confirm his belief that in the absence of well-directed and concentrated research, culture and education tend to get stagnated. To re-orientate the basic concepts of medieval Islamic education and to interpret Islamic History and Philosophy in modern terms could introduce an element of dynamism in the entire field of learning. In the sphere of education, Shibli helped to found the Nadwatul Ulama, at Lucknow, a model institution for teaching of Arabic and Islamic Studies, while in the field of research, he conceived of the plan of Darul Musannefin. An outline of the organization was first published by Maulana Shibli in the Al-Hilal, the well-known weekly of Maulana Abul Kalam Azad. Maulana Shibli had formulated an ambitious plan but all that he could achieve before his death, on November 18, 1914, was to create an endowment of his spacious garden, two kutchcha bungalows and about 300 books to form the nucleus of a library. He had, however, created a small group of co-workers and pupils who could carry the work further and had also compiled a few standard works to serve as pilot project.

The main objectives of Darul Musannefin Shibli Academy are as follows:

- To nurture and sustain a body of scholarly authors.
- To provide a congenial environment for scholars to create, compile and translate literary works of high scholastic and historical value.
- To undertake printing and publication of the literary works of the Academy.

Publications:

Since its very inception, the Academy has been doing very good efforts in the direction of publication of books in the subjects of critical study of Islamic history and other branches of Muslim learning. Over the period of more than nine decades, the Academy had eminently succeeded in meeting these objectives. Inspired by Allama Shibli's personal example and his legacy of well-researched and highly scholarly works, the scholars of the Academy continued to create scholarly works in the fields of Islamic history and literature. The Academy had so far published more than 250 books including such significant works as Seeratun Nabi and Al Faruq. These books by the virtue of their rigorous standards of research are widely acclaimed and continue to be used as reference works.

Following is a list of some very important books which are published by the Academy during past years:

1. Seerat-un-Nabi (Life of the Prophet, pbuh) by Maulana Shibli Nomani
2. Al Faruq (biography of second caliph Umar-Al-Farooq) by Maulana Shibli Nomani
3. Sher-ul-Ajam by Maulana Shibli Nomani (vol. 1-5)
4. Mowazina-i-Anis-o-Dabeer (a masterpiece of literary criticism in Urdu) by Maulana Shibli Nomani
5. Al-Mamoon (Biography of Caliph Mamun-ar-Rasheed) by Maulana Shibli Nomani
6. Seyar-us-Sahaba (the biographies of companions of the Prophet Muhammad, pbuh) by Maulana Shibli Nomani
7. Sher-ul-Hind by Abdus Salam Nadvi (vol. 1-2)

8. Gul-i-Rana by Abdul Hai
9. Seyar-us-Sahaba by Shah Moinuddin Ahmad Nadvi (vol. 1-3)
10. Seerat-us-Sahaba by Maulana Saeed Ansari (vol. 4-5)
11. Seerat-us-Sahaba by Shah Moinuddin Ahmad Nadvi (vol. 6-7)
12. Seerat-us-Sahaba by Maulana Saeed Ansari(vol. 8)
13. Seerat-us-Sahaba by Shah Moinuddin Ahmad Nadvi (vol. 9-11)
14. Ahl-e-Kitaab Sahaba-wa-Tabayeen by Maulana Mujeebullah Nadvi
15. Tabayeen by Shah Moinuddin Ahmad Nadvi
16. Taba Tabayeen by Maulana Mujeebullah Nadvi (vol. 1)
17. Taba Tabayeenby Dr. Mohammad Nayeem Siddiqui Nadvi (vol. 2)
18. Taareekh-e-Islam by Shah Moinuddin Ahmad Nadvi (vol. 1-4)
19. Taareekh Daulat-e-Usmania by Mohammad Uzair (vol. 1-2)
20. Taareekh-e-Saqlia by S. Riyasat Ali Nadvi (vol. 1-2)
21. Taareekh-e-Andalus by S. Riyasat Ali Nadvi (vol. 1)
22. Hamari Badshahi by Abdus Salam Kidwai Nadvi
23. Saleebi Jung by S. Sabahuddin Abdur Rahman
24. Bahadur Khwateen Islam by Syed Suleiman Nadvi
25. Islam Mein Mazhabi Rawadari by S. Sabahuddin Abdur Rahman
26. Taareekh Arzul Quran by Syed Suleiman Nadvi (vol. 1-2)
27. Taleem -ul-Quran by Mohammad Owais Nagrami Nadvi
28. Jama -wa-Tadween Quran by Syed Siddiq Hasan
29. Muqaddamma Ruqqat Alamgeer by S. Najeeb Ashraf Nadvi
30. Bazm-e-Taimuriya by S. Sabahuddin Abdur Rahman (vol. 1-3)

31. Bazm-e-Sufiya by S. Sabahuddin Abdur Rahman
32. Hindustan ke Ahde Wasta ki ek Jhalak by S. Sabahuddin Abdur Rahman
33. Mukhtasr Taareekh-e- Hind by Syed Abu Zafar Nadvi
34. Hindustan ki Kahani by Abdus Salam Kidwai Nadvi
35. Taareekh-e-Sindh by Syed Abu Zafar Nadvi
36. Hindustan ke Ahd-e-Wasta ka Fauji Nizam by S. Sabahuddin Abdur Rahman
37. Hindustan Arabon ki Nazar mein by Ziauddin Islahi (vol. 1-2)
38. Gujarat ki Tamadduni Taareekh by Syed Abu Zafar Nadvi
39. Hindustan ke Musalman Hukmarano ke Tamadduni Jalwe by S. Sabahuddin Abdur Rahman
40. Hindustan ke Musalman Hukmarano ke Tamadduni Jalwe
41. Hindustan ke Salateen, Ulama aur Mashaikh ke Talluqat per ek Nazar by S. Sabahuddin Abdur Rahman
42. Kashmir Salateen ke Ahad Mein translated by Ali Hammad Abbasi
43. Hindustan Ameer Khusroo ki Nazar Mein by S. Sabahuddin Abdur Rahman
44. Zahir-ud-din Mohammad Babur (Hindu Muslim Moarrekheen ki Nazar Mein) by S. Sabahuddin Abdur Rahman
45. Hindustan ki Bazm-e-Rafta ki Sachchi Kahaniyan by S. Sabahuddin Abdur Rahman (vol. 1-2)
46. Islami Uloom -wa-Funoon Hindustan Mein translated by Abul-Irfan Khan Nadvi
47. Hindustan ki Qadim Islami Darsgahein by Abul-Hasanat Nadvi
48. Arab-wa-Hind ke Talluqat by Syed Suleiman Nadvi
49. Hindustan ke Musalman Hukmarano ki Mazhabi Rawadari by S. Sabahuddin Abdur Rahman (vol. 1-3)

50. Ahad-e-Mughalya Mein Hindustan se Muhabbat-wa-Sheeftagi ke Jazbaat by S. Sabahuddin Abdur Rahman
51. Aurangzeb Alamgeer per ek Nazar by Maulana Shibli Nomani
52. A- Ghazzali by Maulana Shibli Nomani
53. Seerat-un- Noman by Maulana Shibli Nomani
54. Seerat Umar bin Abdul Azeez by Maulana Shibli Nomani
55. Seerat Ayesha by Maulana Shibli Nomani
56. Hayat-e-Shibli by Maulana Syed Suleiman Nadvi
57. Imam Razi by Maulana Abdus Salaam Nadvi
58. Hazrat Khwaja Moinuddin Chishti by S. Sabahuddin Abdur Rahman
59. Hazrat Abul Hasan Hajveri by S. Sabahuddin Abdur Rahman
60. Hayat-e-Suleiman by Shah Moinuddin Ahmad Nadvi
61. Maulana Shibli Nomani per ek Nazar by S. Sabahuddin Abdur Rahman
62. Tazkarat-ul-Mohaddesin by Maulana Ziauddin Islahi (vol. 1-3)
63. Mohammad Ali ki yaad mein by S. Sabahuddin Abdur Rahman
64. Yaad-e-Raftagan by Maulana Syed Suleiman Nadvi
65. Bazm-e-Raftagan by S. Sabahuddin Abdur Rahman (vol. 1-2)
66. Sufi Ameer Khusroo by S. Sabahuddin Abdur Rahman
67. Tazkarat-ul-Fuqaha by Umar Siddiq Daryabadi Nadvi
68. Tazkirah Musannefin Hind by Maulana Mohammad Arif Umari
69. Maulana Abul Kalam Azad by Maulana Ziauddin Islahi
70. Swaneh Maulana Roomi by Maulana Shibli Nomani
71. Berkley by Prof. Abdul Bari Nadvi
72. Makalamaat Berkley by Maulana Abdul Majid Daryabadi

73. Fahm-e-Insani by Prof. Abdul Bari Nadvi
74. Ma-aal-wa-Maashiyat by Sahibzadah Zafar Hasan Khan
75. Hukmaye Islam by Maulana Abdus Salaam Nadvi (vol. 1-2)
76. Tabaqat-ul-Umam translated by Qazi Ahmad Mian Akhter
77. Inquilab—ul-Umam by Maulana Abdus Salaam Nadvi
78. Afkaar-e-Asriah translated by Naseer Ahmad Usmani Neotanwi
79. Al-Kalam by Maulana Shibli Nomani
80. Ilm-ul-Kalam by Maulana Shibli Nomani
81. Risalah Ahl-e-Sunnat-wal-Jamaat by Maulana Syed Suleiman Nadvi
82. Maqalat-e-Shibli compiled by Syed Suleiman Nadvi (vol. 1-8)
83. Khutbaat-e-Shibli compiled by Syed Suleiman Nadvi
84. Maqalat-e-Suleiman compiled by S. Sabahuddin Abdur Rahman and Shah Moinuddin Ahmad Nadvi (vol. 1-3)
85. Maqalat-e-Abdus Salam
86. Shizraat-e-Suleiman (vol. 1-3)
87. Makateeb-e-Shibli Compiled by S. Suleiman Nadvi (vol. 1-2)
88. Bareed-e-Firang by Compiled by S. Suleiman Nadvi
89. Mashaheer ke Khutoot (Banaam S. Suleiman Nadvi)
90. Safarnama Rome–wa-Misr-wa-Shaam by Maulana Shibli Nomani
91. Safarnama Afghanistan by S. Suleiman Nadvi
92. Al-Fauz-ul-Azeem (Safarnama Haj) Maulana Habib–ur-Rehman Khan Sherwani
93. Kulliyat Shibli Urdu by Maulana Shibli Nomani
94. Kulliyat Shibli Farsi by Maulana Shibli Nomani
95. Intikhabaat-e-Shibli Compiled by S.Suleiman Nadvi
96. Iqbal-e-Kamil by Maulana Abdus Salam Nadvi
97. Ghalib Madah-wa-Qadah ki roshani mein by S. Sabahuddin Abdur Rahman (vol. 1-2)
98. Sahib-ul-Masnavi by Qazi Talmiz Husain
99. Naqsh-e-Sulaimani by Maulana Abdus Salam Nadvi

100. Khayyam by S. Suleiman Nadvi
101. Mirza Mazhar Jaane-Jaanaan aur unka Kalam by Abdur Razzaq Qureshi
102. Urdu Ghazal by Prof. Yousuf Husain Khan
103. Urdu Zaban ki Tamadduni Ahmiyat by Abdur Razzaq Qureshi
104. Maulana Syed Suleiman ki Deeni-wa-Ilmi Khidmaat by S. Sabahuddin Abdur Rahman
105. Maulana Syed Suleiman ki Tasaneef ka Mutaala by S. Sabahuddin Abdur Rahman
106. Dar-ul-Musannefin ki Tarikh aur Ilmi Khidmaat by khursheed Ahmad Nomani (vol. 1-2)
107. Islam aur Mustashreqeen: Seminar ki Rudaad (vol. 1-6)
108. Taareekh Fiqh Islami translated by Maulana Abdus Salam Nadvi
109. Islami Nizam-e-Taleem by S. Riyasat Ali Nadvi
110. Islam aur Arabi Tamaddun by Shah Moinuddin Ahmad Nadvi
111. Arabon ki Jahaaz-e-Rani by S. Suleiman Nadvi
112. Islam ka Siyasi Nizam by Maulana Mohd. Ishaq Sandelvi
113. Deen-e-Rahmat by Shah Moinuddin Ahmad Nadvi
114. Babari Masjid
115. Mutalleqa Aurat aur Naan-wa-Nafqah by Umair-us-Siddiq Daryadabadi Nadvi
116. Darus-ul-Arab by S. Suleiman Nadvi (vol. 1-2)
117. Al-Risalat-ul-Mohammadiyah translated by Mohammad Nizam Nadvi
118. Al-Islam-wa-al-Musteshreqoon
119. Al-Inteqaad by Maulana Shibli Nomani
120. Suluk-e-Sulemani by Maulana Ashraf Sulemani (vol. 1-2)
121. Shibli Tanqeed ki Roshani mein by S. Shahabuddin Dasnawi
122. Mazameen Maqbool by Prof. Maqbool Ahmad
123. Sada-e-Jaras by Prof. Maqbool Ahmad

124. Tajalliyat Rehmat-e-Alam by Hakim Mohd. Muslehuddin Kazmi
125. Hinduon ki Ilmi-wa-Taalimi taraqqi mein Musalman Hukmarano ki Koshish by Syed Suleiman Nadvi
126. Islamiyat aur Maghrabi Mustashreqeen aur Musalman Musannefin by Syed Abul Hasan Ali Nadvi
127. Quran and Orientalist by Syed Athar Husain
128. Seerat-e-Aisha translated by Syed Athar Husain
129. Shikwah Jawab-e-Shikwah by Altaf Husain & Prof. Maqbool Ahmad
130. Mohammad Shibli Nomani by Jawaid Ali Khan (ICS)

The monthly journal of the Academy, the 'Maarif' is respected for the standard of scholarship and research. It has had few rivals in Urdu language during the last 93 years in respect of quality of its articles and thought contents. It attracted the elite of intellectual life and among its contributors have been writers, authors, poets, theologians and administrators of proven ability.

Renowned Manuscripts

The Library preserves around a total number of 6, 50 manuscripts which are further numbered as 239 in Arabic, 366 in Persian and 20 in Urdu respectively. The estimate of manuscripts has been provided by the present director of the Academy Prof. Ishtiyaq Ahmed Zilli through electronic mail. The Academy has got a significant place for its manuscripts in the database created by National Mission for Manuscripts (NAMAMI). Few important and rare manuscripts belong to the Academy are:

Kulliyat Kalim by Abu Talib Kalim: It is a poetic collection in Persian by an eminent poet Abu Talib Kalim in the court of Mughal emperor Shah Jahan and contains almost all kinds of Urdu verses including Masnavi, Qaseeda and Ghazal. It is composed in 8th Muharram, 1077 A.H. and one of the rarest manuscript of the period mentioned.

Masnavi Mantiq-at-Tair by Farid-ud-din Attar: It is poetic collection of one of the India's most important mystic Khwaja Farid-ud-Din Attar. It is written in Persian and once owned by Bahadur Yar Jung.

Tahreer Aqleedass by Nizam-al-Mulk: Written in Arabic by Nizam-al-Mulk of Tus and contains treatises on Geometry. Though transcriber's name has not mentioned in the manuscript but it was written 1049 A.H.

Sirr-e-Akber by Dara Shikoh: It is Persian translation of Hindu religious book 'Upanishad'. It was translated by none other than Mughal prince Dara Shikoh, who was also having authority over Hindu Religion. Translated in 1068 A.H. and prefixed with picture of one of the important Hindu deity Sri Ganesh Jee.

Akber Namah by Abul Fazal: It is one of the rarest copies of manuscript written by Abul Fazal Allami. It contains beautiful pictures of natural manifestations which are still fresh and without any big change.

Masnavi Futuh-al-Haramain by Maulana Jami: This invaluable manuscript is also written by Jami. Contains not only pictures but it is also one of the masterpiece of the time. The copy of this manuscript is no more available. It is one of the most important manuscripts of the Academy.

Nizam-al-Ghareeb: Written by Ali bin Eisa bin Ibrahim bin Rabayee in 998 A.H. in Arabic. It has transcribed by Sharfuddin. Basically, it is a manuscript of language and grammar and contains a few rare vocabularies.

Automation:

The Darul Musannefin Shibli Academy has developed in its own website even in its awful conditions as far as finance is concerned. Though, the Website contains certain invaluable information about its establishment, aims, publications, Library and other activities carried out by the Academy, but it does not provide any estimation about the printed books and manuscripts collection it preserves at present.

Digitization:

It is hoped that the scholars and other stake holders will be able to see the digital contents of its documents very soon. The Academy has planned to digitize its valuable printed documents including books and manuscripts in near future, as per statement given by its present director.

Other Activities

Apart from the regular works related with publications of books, periodical and preservation and dissemination of its documents, the Academy has also engaged in organization of conferences, symposia and seminars on various themes since its very inception in early twentieth century.

But, during the past few years, due to a combination of factors, the Academy had been facing severe financial problems. Its precarious finances are barely adequate to maintain a skeletal staff on extremely meager remuneration. Modernization of its famed Library, preservation of rare manuscripts, publication of Hindi and English translations of its books and a number of other projects could not be undertaken due to the paucity of funds. Urgent help is needed to enable the Academy to maintain its glorious tradition and continue to serve the community for which it was founded. Launching of a vigorous programme for the publication of famed books of the Academy in accordance with the modern standards is urgently needed. Out of its more than 250 publications, many are out of print and many more are in a very bad condition and need to be republished. The task was taken up in earnest even as the Academy was bereft of necessary resources. During the last two months about twenty books have been published in keeping with the modern requirements.

The library of the Academy houses around 1, 00,000 printed books and 650 manuscripts in its collection. The following table provides a bird eye view of language wise break up of its printed books and manuscripts:

S.No.	*Language*	*Number of Printed Books*	*Number of Manuscripts*
1.	Arabic	--------	239
2.	Persian	-------	366
3.	Urdu	-------	20
4.	Other	-------	25
	Total collection	**1,00,000**	**650**

10. Darul Uloom Nadwatul Ulama, Lucknow

Darul Uloom Nadwatul Ulama, Lucknow

Profile of the Library

Nadwatul Ulama was founded to provide education, training, arts and learning to the people by eminent Ulama (scholars of Islam) in 1894 at Lucknow. It was established on the principle of a balanced synthesis of the classical education with the modern fruits of ICT. Its chief purpose was (a) to evolve a proper integration between the eternal fundamentals of the faith and ever-changing values of human knowledge and learning and (b) to bring about harmony and cohesion among the different groups and schools of thought of Ahl-i-Sunnat Muslims. As, Islamic Sciences are living, evolving and progressive and education was subject to the law of change and reform, hence it was essential that the system of education too, should change and evolve with time for needs of Islamic Millat (Muslim Community).

The layout of a library was always in the mind of its

founders since its very inception. They thought about of a library which will contain a collection of essential printed books, along with the eminent and rare manuscripts and the most distinguished feature which was supposed to be an attractive quality of the library was that it should not be confined to a particular school of thought and instead it could be utilized by everyone who wished to gain the maximum benefit of it. The appeals and articles of Maulana Shibli Nomani and Maulana Abul Kalam Azad published in the newspapers and journals during those days clearly depict that the establishment of this library and its important factor was not supplementary rather it was a very important feature of the objectives and aims of this movement.

The history of this Library began with hearty donation of Maulvi Abdur Rafey, Deputy Collector, who donated nearly 3, 000 books to be a foundation stone and the very first lot for the progression of this Library. Then, Maulvi Abdul Azeem added into this collection by 200 books and Maulvi Syed Abdul Ghani gifted 101 books of literature and history. Few more noble personalities had also donated valuable books to this Library during its initial phase. Other personalities who donated books for its collections are as follows:

- Syed Nawab Ali Hasan Khan
- Maulana Hakeem Syed Abdul Haie Hasani
- Nawab Rasheeduddin Alias Achchey Mian
- Syed Abdul Jaleel
- Syed Wajid Ali
- Maulana Iftikhar Fareedy
- Nawab Syed Najmul Hasan
- Nawab Syed Zuhoorul Hasan
- Dr. Abdullah Abbas Nadwi

- Nisar Ahmad Vakeel Sitapuri
- Hamidullah Khan, District Magistrate, Gonda
- Yousuf-uz-Zaman Farooqui
- Munshi Abdul Ahad, Kolkata
- Maulana Abdul Bari Nadwi
- Hakeem Shakeel Ahmad Shamsi
- Maulana Owais Nagrami Nadwi
- Maulana Munawwar Ali Muhaddis Rampuri
- Masroor Khan Dehlawi
- Abid Suhail Lucknowi
- Dr. Mohammad Iqbal Ansari, Aligarh
- Dr. Syed Luqman Azmi Nadwi
- Ishrat Ali Siddiqui Lucknowi

Dr. Abdullah Abbas Nadwi has also donated a collection of valuable books written by Professor Wali-ul-Haque Ansari which consisted of rare and unparallel hand scripts and printed books. Also many valuable books of Maulana Shibli's personal library having his own signature are the invaluable assets of this Library.

A great number of more than 1,50,000 books possessed by the Library is exposing and denoting the sincerity of the people who have contributed mainly for its collection. Most of the books of the Library are in Arabic language. However, there are many books available in Urdu, English, Turkish, Chinese, French, Pashto, Gujrati, Marathi, Tamil, Sindhi and Malayalam as well. It was initially established in the old office of Nadwatul Ulama at Golaganj, Lucknow. Later, in the year 1908 on recommendation of Maulana Syed Suleiman Nadwi, it was shifted to the glorious Abbasiya Hall of Nadwatul Ulama. Due to its vast collection and scarcity of space here too, a five story building was laid for the library by Sheikh Ahmad Bin Abdul Azeez Ale Mubarak (Chief Justice, UAE) in 1975 under the patronage of Maulana Syed

Abul Hasan Ali Hasani Nadwi. The Library has been working on its two floors since 21st February, 1984.

The number of hand scripts and modern books is continuously increasing. Earlier an old method of cataloguing was prevalent in the Library, which has changed now.

Publications

The Publication Division of Darul Uloom has always been engaged in publishing quality books on Islam in various languages including Arabic, Urdu, Hindi and English. Apart from the books, the Institution has been publishing a number of journals/magazines in Arabic, Urdu, Hindi and English languages for common readers as well as other stakeholders. The following magazines are being published by DUNU:

1. Ar-Raid (Arabic)
2. Al-Bas (Arabic)
3. Tamer-e-Hayat (Urdu)
4. Sachcha Rahi (Hindi)

Renowned Manuscripts

This Library houses some very rare and invaluable manuscripts and hand written documents in its collection.

Following are a few very important and invaluable manuscripts available in the Library:

Al-anwaar-al-Amal-al-Abraar: This complete manuscript deals with the subject of Fiqh (Islamic Jurisprudence) and contains 468 folios. Written by Yusuf bin Ibrahim al-Ardbeli in Naskh calligraphy. The language of the text is Arabic and it is still in good condition.

Al-Khisal-al-Mukaffirah: It is also a complete manuscript in Arabic with only 8 folios on the subject of Sufism (Islamic Mysticism). Written in Naskh by none other than Ibn Hajar al-Askhalani, the great scholar of Islam. It is a paper manuscript and still in good condition.

Al-Asfar al-Arbah: It is a manuscript on various subjects but written by one of the great mystics of Islam Sadr-al-din-al-Shirazi, known as Mulla Sadra. It deals with Islamic Mysticism and Muslim Philosophy. Written in Arabic Nastaliq and contains only one folio.

Tafrih-al-Qulub: It is a paper manuscript on the subject of Sufism (Islamic Mysticism) and contains only 6 folios. Written in Arabic Naskh by M. Bin M. Al-Khitab and scribed by S.Siddiq Hasan Qannauji. It is a complete manuscript from begining to end.

Al-Sahifah: The manuscript is written by Imam Ali bin-al-Husain. It is in Arabic language with Nastaliq calligraphy. Contains 260 folios and complete from begining to end. The subject matter deals with Prayer supplications.

Fata-al-Baqi: It is a manuscript on paper and written by Zakariya bin Yahya al-Ansari in Arabic language in Naskh. The text is in good condition and subject of the text is Hadith. Contains 230 folios and complete from begining to end.

Besides, a nice collection of Arabic manuscripts, the Darul Uloom's Allama Shibli Library also houses around 5, 000 books in Arabic, Persian and Urdu which are unprinted. Few of these, have already been published. However, there are many copies which are still to be printed.

Following is the list of books worthy to mention here:

- Letters of Yaqoob Kindi
- Madinatul-Uloom by Arneequi
- Tazkira (biography) Hafte Aqleem Ameen Razi
- Kashfuz-Zunoon
- Jawahirul Qura'n by Imam Muhammad Al-Ghazzali
- Al Muhakamat (777 H)
- Ejaz Khusravi (735 H)
- Sharah Miftahul Uloom (802 H)

- Sharah Maqasid (840 H)
- Sharah Tawaley (842 H)
- Sihah Jauhari (896 H)
- AL Ieza'h (782 H)
- Zohdatul Asool composed by Sheikh Bahauddin Amili
- Ashiatullamat
- Wafaul Wafa
- Safarnama Nasir Khusroo (1006H)
- AL-Mu'Jamussagheer-Littibrani.
- Kitab-ur-Rooh (an unprinted copy composed by Ummeed Yamani).
- Al Burhan Fi Mutashabihatil Quran by Burhanuddin Abul Qasim Mahmood Bin Hamza Kirmani
- Arabic Deewan of Shah Waliullah Dehlawi
- A Dictionary which bears seal prints of various Mughal kings and a seal of Alamgeer Aurangzeb
- Muntahal-Uloom Fi Tafseere Kitabillahil Hayyil Qayyum
- Deewan-e-Muntazir (the virtuous student of Mushafi)
- Deewan-e- Brahman
- Deewan-e- Mushafi
- Shahnama Urdu
- Deewan-e- Shaida
- Deewan-e- Saba
- Mahar Jahan Taab
- Tazkira Meer Hasan
- Graphic copies of Shahnama of Firdausi
- Graphic copy of Ajaibul Makhlooqat
- Famous commentary of Allama Nooruddin Basari
- Takhmeesat of Shah Abdul Aziz and Shah Rafiuddeen
- Ilm-ul-Tafsir by Jalaluddin Suyuti

- Adatus-Sabireen-wa-Zakheeratush-Shakireen by Ibn Qayyim-al-Jauzi.
- Isa Ghauji by Athir-al-Din-al-Abhari
- Ajab-al-Tarikh by Habibullah Qandhari
- Abiyat-i-Mukhtalifah
- Risalah Fi-al-Ashhar-al-Haram by Mulla Ali Qari
- Fatawa Ibn Taimiyah by Ahmad bin Abdul Halim Ibn Taimiyah
- Nil al-Aum□ar min Asrar-i Mantiqi al-Akhbar by Muhammad bin Ali Shokani
- Al-Hadyat al-Shahjahaniyah by M. Shams al-Din al-Qannauji
- Al-Siraj-al-Munir by Mufti Tabai-al-Lucknowi
- Ayyuhal-Walad by Muhammad bin Muhammad Ghazzali
- Risalah-fi-Anfaq by Ibn Qayyim al-Jauziyah
- Al-Shams-al-Bazighah by Mulla Mahmud Jaunpuri
- Risalah Irshad al-Saalikin by Sharaf-al-Din Ahmad Munairi
- Sikander Namah by Nizami Ganjwi
- Tadaad-i-Surah-i-Kalam Allah.

Automation

The Institute has maintained a very informative website which contains almost all relevant information about its establishment, aims, courses, collection and other infrastructure. The Institute has maintaining its website in Arabic, Urdu and English. It is being felt from a long time that the Library is in need to be rearranged and it should be equipped with the modern facilities. So, the new and fresh set up of the Library was prepared and demonstrating a good taste and deep interest of modernization, the Library has been computerized covering all the inclusion of the library after a hard and laborious work of many years. It will help all the research works in every respect and any one can easily access any desired information about the books or the inclusion of the library. The system has been computerized in such a way that complete information regarding all the books of Arabic, English, Persian, Hindi and Urdu etc (Author's name, publication year, accession number, index etc.) can be displayed on the screen of the computer any time when required. This is really a big work which is not less than an adventure and has probably the first work of its kinds and status been attended in the library of any Islamic Institution considered as important as that of the Darul Uloom Nadwatul Ulama.

In the same way a page wise micro film of the unprinted book has also been made to be screened. A CD copy of the desired book is being provided to those who are busy with the research works in order to facilitate them fulfil their tasks.

Digitization

Though, the digitization work has not been started here, but there is an urgent need to digitize the library collection particularly rare manuscripts and unprinted documents for a wider and global access. Digitization will definitely help the Academy for popularization of its vast collection ans accessibility.

Other Activities

Apart from the academic programmes and other related works, the Institution is also organizing seminars, symposia and lectures on various themes from time to time for the benefit of students and staff mebers.

Government Oriental Manuscript Library and Research Centre (GOML&RC), Chennai

11. Government Oriental Manuscript Library and Research Centre (GOML&RC), Chennai

Profile of the Library

The Government Oriental Manuscripts Library and Research Centre, Chennai is a radically distinctive library which consists of a rich trove of manuscripts of works in Literature, History, Philosophy and Science, written in south Indian and oriental languages, and of Kaifiyats, a distinguished literary genre and inscriptions found in many places belonging to different periods of history. The Library is a government body governed by the curator under the aegis of the director of Archaeology, government of Tamil Nadu. Although, the Library grew from time to time it came into vogue in the literal sense since 1869 and is located in the premises of the Madras University Library.

The Library mainly comprises of the collections of Colonel Mackenzie, Dr. Leyden and Mr. C.P. Brown. The main objective of the Library is to acquire and preserve manuscripts. It also helps in classification and cataloguing of manuscripts, apart from the publication of rare manuscripts and library catalogues is also one of its activity areas. The Library also engages in purchase of books and periodical for reference, and accelerates supply of authentic information in respect to manuscripts to the scholars. The following main special collection of the Library includes:

- Mackenzie's Collection
- Leyden's Collection
- Brown's Collection

Publications:

GOML&RC has brought out four hundred fifty eight publications so far in regional languages like Sanskrit, Urdu, Arabic, Persian and Marathi languages including descriptive and triennial catalogues of its manuscripts in many languages. It has also published thirty volumes of Tamil manuscripts, fifty three volumes of Sanskirit manuscripts and twenty eight volumes of Telugu manuscripts. The multilingual bulletin published annually by GOML&RC contains in-print, rare and unpublished manuscripts in various languages. Twenty one volumes have been published so far. Its publicationshas been brought under two series.

(i) Government Oriental Manuscript Series, and

(ii) Government Oriental Series.

Renowned Manuscripts

From such a small beginning, GOML&RC, Chennai, has grown to its present dimensions and it possesses 72,314 manuscripts dealing with Mathematics, Astronomy, Sidhdha, Ayuerveda, Unani, Vedas, Agama, Music, Architecture, Fine Arts, History and many other subjects written in Tamil, Sanskirit, Marathi, Urdu, Arabic and Persian languages.

The noteworthy manuscripts available in the Library are as follows:

Uttara Kalamrita : It is a refrence work on Vedic Astrology or Jyotisa, written by Kalidasa. However, it is not known whether Kalidasa who wrote this work is the same Kalidasa who wrote Raghuvamsha and Abhijnana Sakuntalam. The manuscript is available in various libraries in India including the Government Oriental Manuscript Library and Research Centre in Chennai. The text was first produced in the Telugu script. The reference to Andhra Bhasha, Urdu or Persian, Turushka, Sukkani, Rahu Kala, and other things show that he came after the sixteenth century. The Uttara Kalamrita contains a wealth of astrological principles which are derived from earlier works on Astrology namely Brihat Parashara, Hora Shastra, Brihat Jataka and Phaladeepika.

Ramayana: It is a manuscript in Sanskirit language with Telugu script and written by Valmiki. Though, it is incomplete in nature but very important text as a religious scripture. Contains 319 folios.

Ramacarita: The manuscript deals with poetical verses in Sanskirit language. The script of the text is Devanagri and unfortunately, it is also an incomplete manuscript.

Ramayana Vyakhya: It is a complete manuscript written by Govinda Raj. The manuscript deals with interpretation of Ramayana and contains 114 folios.

Goladipika: It is a complete manuscript written by Paramesevara and available in Sanskirit language. The subject of the manuscript is Grantha. It is a paper manuscript and contains 16 folios.

Ramamantra: The manuscript is also known as Malamantra. The subject of the manuscripts is Mantra and written in Telugu. It is a paper manuscript and complete from beginning to end.

Apart from the above mentioned manuscripts, the Institute houses following some very important manuscripts in its collection:

- Talacandrika by Maudgayavirupaksa
- Jnanadipika by Visvanatha
- Yajnavalkyasmrti by Yajnavalkya
- Gulzar-i-Matam by Sayyid Muhammad Hasan bin Sayyid Haider
- Badai al-Insha by Mulla Yusufi
- Diwan-i Fitrat by Mir Muizz al-Din Musawî Khan Fitrat
- Risalah-i-Fiqh by Muhammad Yaqoob
- Madhhab-i-Ishq by Nihal Chand Lahori
- Hasiyah Abd Allah Yazdi by Najm-al-Din bin Abd Allah Yazdi
- Mathnawi Mir Taqi Mir (Vol. II) by Mir Taqi Mir
- Diwan-i-Wali by Wali Aurangabadi

- Mathnawi Mirat-al-Anwar by Shah Wali-Allah Qadri
- Taqwiyat-i-Burhani by Dilawar Husain Faruqi-al-Nasiri
- Jawami-al-Kalim by Ali bin Hasan-al-din al-Muttaqi.

Automation

The GOML&RC has its own well established website portal on which almost all relevant information about its collection, manuscripts preservation, and publications accompanied with events provided in a systematic way. The Online Public Access Catalogue (OPAC) of the Library is not accessible through Internet.

Digitization

The process of digitizing rare manuscripts and priceless books is still in infancy in this Library. Under the National Mission for Manuscripts programme 1,880 Sidhdha manuscripts in Tamil language has already been digitized. Under the state and central government shared scheme for the year 2009-2010 (plan) a total number of Rs. 4, 6,666/-have been approved for purchasing computer accessories ,related software, lamination and digital camera for this organization. In this connection, an amount of Rs. 3, 50, 00/- has been sanctioned by government of India as its share and State share will be released shortly. The Government Oriental Manuscript Library and Research Centre, now housed in Madras University Campus, will be shifted to the new Anna Centenary Memorial Library Complex at Kottupuram after completion.

There is an urgent need to speed up the digitization process through which a wide range of people will be able to access the treasures of this great Institution. This will be done on priority basis due to immense demand for manuscripts preserved in this Library from scholars and students from all over the world. As, the Library holds many priceless oriental collections of printed books and manuscripts, therefore, scholars and other stakeholders are visiting to make use of the resources of the Library daily both from the country and abroad.

Other Activities

From the earliest days, the Library is a tradition of displaying its rare and valuable manuscripts for the benefit of scholars and clienteles. The rare and priceless manuscripts of GOML&RC were displayed in the manuscript exhibitions on the following occasions:

- ·1964 - The Twenty Sixth International Congress of Orientalist in New Delhi.
- ·1964 - The Third All India Agama Silpa Bharata Folklore Conference in Kancheepuram
- ·1965 - The World Telugu Conference in Hyderabad
- ·1968 - The Second World Tamil Conference in Madras.
- ·1968 - The Lord Mahaveera's 25th Parinirvana Centenary Celebrations in Madras
- ·1980-The Silver Jubilee Celebrations of the Sanskrit Department Vivekananda College in Madras
- ·1980 - The Chitirai Festival in Madurai
- ·1981 - The Fifth World Tamil Conference in Madurai
- ·1982 - Seminar on Sanskrit Literature at Vivekananda College in Madras

Total holdings of printed books and manuscripts of the Library are 25,373 and 72,314 respectively. The language wise break up of printed books as well as manuscripts of the Library is enumerated here which reflects the proportions of oriental documents shared by a variety of languages of India:

S.No.	*Language*	*Number of Printed Books*	*Number of Manuscripts*
1.	Telugu	1875	2,150
2.	Sanskrit	7320	48,884
3.	Tamil	5442	16,398
4.	Kannada	700	250
5.	Marathi	137	956

S.No.	*Language*	*Number of Printed Books*	*Number of Manuscripts*
6.	Malayalam	444	------
7.	Hindi	130	------
8.	Bengali	18	-----
9.	Arabic	230	407
10.	Persian	265	------
11.	Urdu	705	184
12.	English	6926	-------
13.	French,German and European languages	194	------
14.	Dictionaries	182	------
15.	Catalogues	805	-------
16.	Other Oriental Languages		127
17.	Local Records	-------	434
	Total Collection	**25,373**	**72,314**

11. Hazrat Pir Mohammed Shah Library, Ahmadabad, Gujarat

Profile of the Library

Hazrat Pir Mohammed Shah was born in 1689, in the Bijapur city of Karnataka. Pir Mohammad Shah was a Hussaini Sayyed and a well-respected Sufi who lived in Ahmadabad during the rule of Mughal emperor Aurangzeb. His parents emigrated from the holy city of Medina and settled in Bijapur. The Pir memorized the Holy Quran at the young age of seven and became an accomplished Qari (reciter of Holy Quran), performed Haj at the age of twelve and thereafter stayed in Medina for several years pursuing higher learning. He spent his adolescent years visiting great centers of learning in the Islamic world and paying homage at the Dargah (tomb-shrine) of the saints. He later returned to his home at Bijapur and from there moved to Ahmadabad. The Pir was a great lover of learning and possessed an extraordinary memory powers. Pir Mohammad Shah was a bi-lingual poet himself and wrote profusely in Persian and Dakhani. Among his many works, the best known is *Nur-ush-Shuyukh* in Persian which is versified history in the *Mutaqarib* meter. During his lifetime, the Pir and his *Murids (disciples)* had amassed a huge collection of manuscripts and books of great academic and spiritual value. These are housed in the *Kutubkhana (library)*. He was died in the year 1749.[23]

The Hazrat Pir Mohammed Shah Library is located in Ahmadabad, in the state of Gujarat, India. One of the oldest libraries in India and has a collection of rare original manuscripts in Arabic, Persian, Urdu, Sindhi and Turkish languages. The Library is located within the precincts of the tomb-shrine complex of Hazrat Pir Muhammad Shah. The Library has a treasure trove of over 10,000 books in Arabic, Persian, Urdu, and English covering diverse subjects. The trustees have prepared microfilms and photocopies of some rare books.

Publications

The Pir Muhammad Shah Dargah Sharif Trust Library, Ahmadabad has published a descriptive catalog entitled "Arabi, Farsi, Urdu Makhtutat ki Wadahati Fihrist" in five volumes in 1998.

Renowned Manuscripts

This Library has over 2, 000 original manuscripts in Arabic, Persian, Urdu, Sindhi and Turkish, which are 700 to 800 years old. Many of them contain hand written explanatory notes along the margins by the Pir himself. Few important manuscripts titles are worthy to mention here:

Mahabharata: This manuscript is the translation of Mahabharata in Persian by a Wada Agar Brahmin who worked in the courts of the Mughal rulers.

Divan-e-Kalim: It is a poetic collection in Persian language and authored by Abu Talib Kalim Kashani in the year 1061 A.H. The collection contains 390 poems and 27 tetrastiches.

Dhakirat-al-Muluk: This manuscript authored by Mir sayyid Ali Bin Shahbuddin Hamadani in Persian language written in 1108 A.H. The collection deals with the administration of homeland, ethics and maintenance of residence. Basically covers detailed rules and regulations of governance and adminstration of the State and role of officers or rulers in it.

Tarikh-e-Bengala: This Persian language manuscript covers historical perspectives and composed by none other than Hatifi. Transcribed by Pundit Nand Lal Kowl and written in the year 1279 A.H. Basically dealing with the history of Bengal beginning with the death of Ali Vardi Khan alias Mahabat Jung and concludes with the death of Shuja-ud-Daula. It is one of the lesser known manuscripts on the history of Bengal.

Shafi-al-Maani: The manuscript is written by Shafi-ud-din Ibn Evad Lucknowi and transcribed by Hazrat Pir Mohammad Shah himself and Mazhar Ali. It is in Persian language using Nastaliq script and written in the year 1250

A.H. Basically it is a lexicon and a few beginning pages has been damaged. It is a rare manuscript on lexicon and arranged alphebitally with notes in the margin.

Fusus-ul-Hekam: It is a one of the most important treatise on Islamic Mysticism composed by the great Muslim mystic and philospher, Sheikh Mohi-ud-Din Ibn Al-Arabi. Written in Arabic and clear Naskh on paper and contains 400 folios. It is a complete manuscript without any damage or missing elements.

Apart from the above mentioned manuscripts, the Library also possess following very important text in its collection:

- A copy of the hand written Holy Quran by Mughal king Aurangzeb.
- Radha Krishna Geet (translated into Persian)
- Al-Biruni
- Anis-al-Ghuraba by Nur Muhammad
- Anis-al-Ghuraba by Nur Qutb Alam Pandwi
- Anis-al-Muttaqin by Abd-al-Samad Faqih Hasan Bin Faqih Muhammad.
- Anis-al-Mutlaq by Nur Muhammad Shaikh Adam bin Shaikh.
- Irshadat-e-Hamidi by Hamid
- Minhaj-ul-Abidin by Abu Hamid Bin Muhammad Ghazzali
- Kashf-ul-Awalim by Majhul
- Haqq Numa by Dara Shikoh
- Sharah Gulshan-e-Razz by Muhammad Bin Safar Sherwani
- Gulistan by Shaikh Sadi
- Risalah Jununiya by Sayyed Abdul Majid

Automation

Though, till date, the Library has not developed its own website but relevant information about its rare collections can be obtained through Internet. The National Archives of India in its second meeting for the year 2010-2011, held on 2, December, 2010, has sanctioned a total grant of Rs. 1,40,000/- for preservation of manuscripts and rare books to this Library. The said amount is further divided into following heads for better preservation of valuable manuscripts and printed documents of the Library:

- An approximate amount of Rs. 1,00,000/- allocated for cataloguing of manuscripts of Persian and Arabic books and their editing, assessing, deciphering, etc.
- An amount of Rs. 30,000/-for remuneration of Experts Services towards preservation and conservation of manuscripts.

For purchase of a few steel cupboards for storing of manuscripts and books an amount of Rs. 10,000 has already been allocated by the above mentioned organisation.

The titles with essential bibliographic details of its manuscripts can be viewed at manuscripts database developed by National Mission for Manuscripts (NAMAMI) on Mission's official website.

Digitization

It is fact that digital preservation has unmatched benefits compare to traditional forms but at the same time it is a costly and expensive venture. It seems that, the organization under consideration has not been developed any kind of Digital Library of its own yet. But, it is hoped that, in foreseeable future one can make use of its valuable assets in a digital format.

Other Activities

The Kutubkhana (Library) has a small museum displaying various belonging of the Pir, some of the ancient manuscripts and a human-size candle brought here from Makkah. The Pir Mohammad Shah Library is considered one of its kinds in western part of India, a treasure trove waiting to be discovered by lovers of Islamic Sciences, literature and art.

Khuda Bakhsh Oriental Public Library, Patna

12. Khuda Bakhsh Oriental Public Library, Patna

Profile of the Library

The Khuda Bakhsh Oriental Public Library is a unique repository of about 21,000 manuscripts and 2, 50,000 printed books in major oriental languages of India. Though founded earlier, it was opened for public in October, 1891 by Khan Bahadur Khuda Bakhsh with 4,000 manuscripts, of which he inherited 1,400 from his father Maulvi Mohammed Bakhsh. Khuda Bakhsh Khan donated his entire personal collection to the people of Patna by a deed of trust. Acknowledging the immense historical and intellectual value of its rich and valuable collection, the government of India declared the library as an institution of national importance by an act of Parliament in 1969. The Library is now fully funded by the Ministry of Culture, Government of India. Since July 1970 onwards, it has been granted an autonomous affiliation under the Department of Culture, Ministry of Tourism and Culture, Government of India, with the governor of Bihar as its Ex-Officio Chairman.[24]

Today, the Khuda Bakhsh Oriental Public Library houses a very nice collection of about 230 original paintings of Mughal, Rajput, Oudh, Iranian and Turkish schools. The Library also possesses a sizeable number of original letters of eminent personalities and coins of kings and emperors of India.[25]

It is considered as one of the richest public libraries of India as far as oriental collection of manuscripts and printed documents are concerned. Besides fulfilling the need of the research scholars and academics, the Library also publishes various literatures from time to time on Indology, Religions, and Medieval Indian History etc. The Library takes step in translating the rare volumes of the past into Urdu, Arabic and Persian. It occasionally organizes seminars, lectures and conferences etc. on a range of themes including Religion, Culture, Literature etc. It, being the largest oriental public library in the country is in the process of computerizing its many services to provide better prospect in making use of its valuable collections of rare manuscripts and printed documents.

Publications

A very special feature of Khuda Bakhsh Oriental Public Library is its publications which have created history in the intellectual world. Since 1977, it has been issuing regularly a multi-lingual research quarterly journal entitled Khuda Bakhsh Library Journal. The basic aim of bringing out this journal is to move forward research in Oriental and Islamic Studies and also to promote research in languages and literature. Hence, it includes scholarly articles, reprints of articles from old research periodicals and prints original articles on the subjects in which the Library specializes, the periodical has an impact on the research on the above mentioned subjects. The Journal has been in active publication from 1977 and around 127 issues have come out so far. These journals contain articles in Urdu, English, Hindi, and Persian and even in Arabic. Wide range of articles covered by this journal includes:

- Tibb (Unani Medicine)
- Tasawwuf (Islamic Mysticism)
- Islamic Studies
- History
- Literature
- Biographies
- Comparative Religion
- Texts of Rare Manuscripts and Old Prints
- Facsimile Edition of Rare Materials
- Selections from Urdu Periodicals
- Indices
- Documents on Contemporary Islam
- Proceedings and Papers of Khuda Bakhsh Seminars
- Thought-provoking writings on contemporary Indian Islam
- Articles on various dimensions of Indo-Islamic Culture
- Manuscriptology

Simultaneously, the Library also undertook a project of publishing research treatises, its manuscripts after getting them edited by scholars, facsimile edition of manuscripts, indices of Urdu periodicals, catalogue of the manuscripts, books bridging the communal gap and also books on Indian Culture, History, Literature and Islam. It has brought out about 400 titles in Arabic, Hindi, English, Persian and Urdu languages so far. These journals have been serving the need of its readers for last 35 years and they are perhaps the only source of articles which are so difficult to get by through any other publication in India.

About thirty collections of manuscripts and books have so far been acquired as donation from the owners in addition to those purchased by the Library. The printed collection has, on the other hand, its own value covering a wide spectrum of subjects such as Memoirs, Biographies, Tibb(Unani Medicine), Hinduism and other oriental topics in English, Arabic, Persian, Urdu and Hindi, etc. One significant part of this collection is the Periodical Section which contains around 35,000 bound volumes of old and new periodicals. It is very much used by the scholars and even a general person can go through it by paying a visit to the Library. Hence, the Publications Division is one of the most important divisions of this great Library.

Renowned Manuscripts:

Preservation and conservation of manuscripts in multiple languages is one of the most essential tasks of any kind of a public library. This library is no exception in collecting and preserving the glorious past with the help of ancient and medieval era manuscripts. The Library has already published 36 volumes of descriptive catalogue of manuscripts covering an approximate of one third of total collection of its manuscripts. During the year 2008-09, the Library has undertaken repairing and chemical treatment of thousands of manuscripts and books and great number of books/ manuscripts were fumigated. 2,007 manuscripts/books were fumigated and 36,469 folios of manuscripts/books were repaired and given curative preservation. The Library has acquired 5 manuscripts, 5,000 books, 69 periodicals and 169 audio & video cassettes in its annual collection. 10 monograph and 3 issues of journal have been published during the period under review. The work of digitization of manuscripts which was started in September, 2005 has been completed with pilot project of 10, 00,000 folios during the period under review.[26]

The Library preserve following exceptionally important and famous manuscripts in its collection:

Diwan-e-Hafiz: It is an anthology of the ghazals or lyrics of the renowned Persian poet of the 14th century A.D, Hafiz of Shiraz. Hafiz is universally acknowledged as the finest composer of Persian lyrics, lyrics that have significant mystic content. An interesting fact about the 'Diwan' is that it has been consulted by credulous persons for obtaining 'faals' , that is, to plumb the secret of the fate. Consequebtly, the text is very popular. Though, there is no dearth of this manuscript in the World, but one copy from fifty copies in this Library is very unique because at one time, it was in the possession of Mughal emperors and it contains marginal notes in the handwriting of atleast two of them-Humayun and Jahangir.

Tarikh-e-Khandan-e-Timuriyah: The Tarikh-e-Khandan-e-Timuriyah is a richly illustrated and the only extant copy of a manuscript which deals with the history of Timur and his descendants in Iran and India, including the Mughal rulers Babur, Humayun and Akbar. The manuscript was compiled during 1577-78 A.D., in the reign of Akber.

The manuscript is remarkable for the number and splendor of its illuminations, all representing that delicate and highly refined style that was the trademark of the important artists of the imperial atelier under Akbar's patronage. Some of the miniatures contain the names of the painters. A total of 51 artists including the leading masters of the time like Daswant, Miskin, Madho Mukund, Haidar Kashmiri, Miskeen, Manohar and Basawan have been mentioned. Most of them have been included by Abul Fazal in his list of eminent artists at Akbar's court. In most cases, more than one artist has worked on some of the 133 paintings contained in the manuscript. Sieges and battles comprise the principal themes of the paintings, as may be expected of a chronicle of generations of conquerors and rulers.

The manuscript is written in beautiful bold Nastaleeq, within coloured and gold-ruled borders. The paper is of an excellent quality, of a sharp cream colour and with a slight ivory gloss.

Due to its importance, it has been recorded in the Memory of the World Register at 2010-62.

Kitab-al-Hashish: The first of its manuscripts treasures in Arabic is Kitab-al-Hashish. It relates to medicinal plants and herbs. It is the Arabic translation of the Materia and Medica of Pedasius Dioscortides, the botanist of Cilicia during the days of the Roman emperor Nero. A soldier by profession in his younger days, Dioscortides travelled over a wide area extending from Greece through Asia Minor into Gaul. He collected hundreds of plants and herbs in the course of his travels and also obtained detailed information on their medicinal properties. The book is based on his personal observations and experiences.

Kitab-al-Tasreef: The second text identified as a manuscript treasure is the Kitab-al-Tasreef, a text dealing with surgery in particular. It enjoys the distinction of being one of the earliest illustrated texts on the science of surgery, containing a fairly large number of coloured sketches of surgical instruments. Many of these, in spite of rather crude shapes, bear a striking resemblance to some of the surgical instruments being used in modern times. The author, Abul Qasim bin Abbas-al- Zahrawi was a renowned surgeon of the 11th century A.D.

The book consists of thirty chapters and is divided into two volumes. The first deals with general principles of medicine; the second and more important deals with tools and techniques of surgery. The Khuda Bakhsh manuscript was transcribed in 1190 A.D. It has 240 folios, written in ornamental Naskh. It is among those rare manuscripts which came to this Library from Cordova. Significantly, this work has been translated and published at several earlier occasions. Its first translation in Latin was published at Venice in 1497. A French translation followed in 1861. More recently, an English translation has been published in 1973.

Mirat-al-Quds: This manuscript transcribed some four hundred years back in the city of Agra in the reign of Mughal king Akber. It bears the title Mirat-al-Quds or the Holy Mirror. Contains a biography of Jesus Christ together with his teachings based on the Gospels. It has 179 folios with fourteen lines at each page. It is written in beautiful Nastaleeq characters within gold and coloured borders.

A few other exceptionally renowned manuscripts in the collection are:

·Sirat-e-Firoz Shahi

- Jahangir Namah
- Badshah Namah (includes finest paintings of Mughal School)
- Umdatul Kalam Fi Bayan-al-Halal-wal-Haram written by Abdul Khaliq Ajmairi
- Elaj bi Asmaey-Ilahi (Cures by names of Almighty God)
- Elaj bid Dua (Cures by Prayers)
- Ilm-al-Faraiz by Ahmadi
- Ilm-Faraiz by mufti Inayat Ahmed Kakowi
- Aishun-Nabi
- Amaliyat-i-Qurani
- Aqaid-i-Sharfi by Sharf-al-Din-Bihari
- Aqaid Ahl-i-Tashee by Nawab Ali Hadi
- Aqaid Namah by Sakhawat Ali Jaunpuri
- Aina Tareekh-i-Hind by Qaiser Amrohavi Sayyed Mahmud Hasan
- Unwan-al-Muraqqasaat-wal Mutarrabaat by Ali Ibn Abi Imam Musa.

A folio of mss. Diwan-i-Hafiz, KBOPL, Patna (courtesy: NAMAMI)

Two folios of mss. Kita-al-Tasrif, KBOPL, Patna (courtesy: NAMAMI)

Two folios of mss. Tarikh-i-Khandan Timuriyah, KBOPL, Patna (courtesy: NAMAMI)

Automation:

Modernization was introduced in the Library as early as 1950s with the provision of reprographic services. Other equipments for further modernization and improvement of library services were added gradually.

A small Conservation Lab is attached to the rare collection for fumigation, deacidification, lamination and binding. This is to be modernized with latest equipments supported with Fumigation Chamber with latest techniques and Impregnator. Latest and sophisticated machines are also acquired for quality binding.

In late 1980s, four computers and a Laser Printer were purchased with Urdu, Hindi and English software to help to carry out the entire Desk Top Publishing (DTP) work in-house to speed up printing and also to create a database of accessioning record of printed material in order to check the duplication of books. To computerize the entire Library Stock and provide online service, a major project was prepared in consultation with National Informatics Centre (NIC), Delhi and Patna and submitted to the Department of Culture for approval. With the generous grant from DOC, a Computer Centre was set up in 1999.

This was one of the major events coming on heels of the dawn of the new century. This Computer Centre is equipped with the following items:

- XEON Server
- Modern Pentium based systems (22 Nos.)
- Color Laser Jet Printer
- Laser Jet Printers
- Photo Printer
- Office Jet All-in-One
- Scanner
- Digital Camera

All the computer systems and peripherals have been interconnected through LAN for better sharing of resources. The Library has also taken a Broadband connection through which Internet and e-mail facilities are available. This facility will soon be extended to research scholars. The pilot project of retro-cataloguing of 15,000 (10 000 English and 5000 Urdu, Hindi and Persian) books was completed in 2003-04.[27]

Under its modernization project, the Library has already developed its own website with the technical assistance of NIC. Entire collection of catalogue has been fully scanned and published with collaboration of NIC, Bihar Unit and available both on its website as well in CD-ROM format. The descriptive catalogue of the Library collection is available in 30 volumes set which appeared in 1923 and was reprinted in 1970s. Print catalogues were converted into Machine Readable Format (MARC) by NICNET, which has undertaken the digitization project.[28]

Now, the Institution has launched a website and a link is given to the whole catalogue of the Library in a tabular form. The table has hyperlinks to different volume of the catalogue which can be browsed as JPEG files and browsed from as a file from top to bottom. The whole project has taken by National Informatics Centre. It has not introduced any retrieval mechanism as the document is treated as collection of image file in JPEG format. The catalogue ironically cannot be accessed under metadata or any useful descriptors.

The bibliographic details of manuscripts can be viewed on the manuscripts database of National Mission for Manuscript's (NAMAMI) website.

Digitization

The Khuda Bakhsh Oriental Public Library has initiated digitization of Arabic and Persian Manuscripts of the Medieval India.[29] All the Initial formalities with regard to digitization of the manuscripts of the Library have been done during the year 2003-04.[30]

The pilot project of digitization of 10, 00,000 pages of manuscripts has been entrusted to NICSI and the work was started in October, 2005. Some 400 thousand pages are now available. Documents are accessible as JPEG files. Digitization of descriptive catalogue of manuscripts has already been completed and it has been published over the Internet for global dissemination.[31]

As the Library is now all set to digitize (change the data into digital form) its sizable collection of Urdu, Persian, Arabic, Hindi, Sanskrit, Pali and Turkish manuscripts and rare printed material on oriental and Islamic Studies in the sub-continent, therefore, a two-day workshop had been organized at the Library to discuss the various aspects of digitization and scanning of manuscripts to have full assessment of the technicalities of the job and its implications. The workshop was inaugurated and presided by Patna High Court Judge Justice Aftab Alam and former Vice Chancellor of Patna University, Nazre Ahsan, respectively. While highlighting the importance of manuscripts, he said that, these manuscripts have become unusable with the passage of time and to avoid further damage to these precious collections and save them from being frequently exposed to the heat and light of microfilming cameras, digitization had become necessary. Ahsan said that, the digitization would be the most rapid mode for the users to get access to a large number of rare manuscripts, which are of great interests to scholars of Arabic, Persian, Turkish and even Central Asian Republics. A large number of technical experts, computer agencies, library scientists and scholars were participated in the workshop.[32]

MRC of National Mission for Manuscripts started functioning since September, 2003 and has collected information on **27,820** manuscripts with electronic data. The 20 publicity campaigns organized by the Centre have yielded rich results in terms of creating awareness in the people in preserving their manuscripts and in sharing the information.

The Library has been part of the MCC of the Mission since September 2003. They have identified partner centers and are extending assistance in preventive and curative conservation activities. They MCC have already provided preventive conservation for 1, 69, 502 and curative conservation for 37, 033 manuscripts folios covering 14 institutions till date.[33]

In the view of the importance of the manuscripts preserved in this Library and elsewhere in the vicinity of Patna, the National Mission of Manuscripts has selected Khuda Bakhsh Oriental Public Library, Patna as nodal agency for the Mission of digitization of manuscripts in Bihar state. The MRC of National Mission for Manuscripts at KBOPL, Patna concentrates mainly on documenting Urdu, Arabic, and Persian manuscripts. The MRC, started in September 2003 has collected information on **23,144** manuscripts with electronic data. For the survey, it has covered 65 government institutions and 117 private collections in twenty-seven districts. The 13 publicity campaigns organized by the Centre have yielded rich results in terms of creating awareness in the people in preserving their manuscripts and in sharing the information. The Survey has evoked very positive response from the community, and resulted in the documentation of hitherto unknown manuscripts.

Other Activities:

Khuda Bakhsh Library is not merely a library; it is in fact a nucleus of multi-dimensional activities. It caters to the needs of intellectuals and scholars, promotes research, advocates communal harmony and also serves public. During the last fifty years, it has organized about 200 extension lectures, talks, group discussions and debates. Eminent personalities have delivered lectures on a variety of subjects. International seminars have been organized on manuscript literature on Tibb (Unani Medicine), Tasawwuf (Islamic Mysticism), Quranic Sciences, and Medieval Indian history followed by the seminars on Urdu manuscripts and on Indo-Uzbek relations. 'Free India' and 'Dr. Zakir Husain' were the topics for national seminars. Besides, symposia on Reservation for Muslims and Indian Woman have also been arranged in the Library. Several talks have been organised on Health Care and Hygiene especially for public awareness. The Library also arranges National and International Mush'aira's (Urdu Poetry Recitation), Kavi Sammelans (Hindi Poetry Recitation) and Qawwalis (a unique kind of Urdu poetry) besides Film shows representing Indian Culture and also documentaries.

The founder of this library, Khuda Bakhsh, struggled throughout his life for communal harmony. The Library, thus, represents this quality of the founder through its collection and holds group discussions on the issue. The Library encourages scholars and provides them all research facilities including free accommodation. It awards 10 research fellowships - 3 Senior and 7 Junior - for a period of 2 years and helps them to pursue Ph.D./D.Litt. It also assigns different projects to them, for example, editing of manuscripts, compilation of descriptive catalogue of manuscripts, indices of Urdu periodicals, subject bibliographies, etc.

Besides, it also offers lump sum amount to retired professors to work on its rare manuscripts. Compilation of descriptive catalogue of manuscripts is also a research work. The catalogues published so far, contain rich information about the manuscripts and hence they are highly valued in the academic world.

The Organisation has so far published 36 volumes of descriptive catalogue of manuscripts covering about one-third of the total collection. Moreover, the hand-list of manuscripts in Arabic (3 vols.), Persian (3 vols.) and Urdu (1 volume) have also been compiled and printed for the benefit of the readers. More volumes of descriptive catalogue are likely to be published soon. Khuda Bakhsh Library was well on its way to become the country's first public library to Internet in fulfilment of the wishes of Pundit Jawaharlal Nehru which he penned down in the Visitor's Book during his visit to the Library on Nov. 1, 1953 in these words – 'I should like to see them reproduced by the latest techniques, so that others can see them and share in this joy'.

Contributions of Maulvi Khuda Bakhsh Khan to the society as a whole have been immense. To pay homage to this great soul devoted to human cause and to commemorate his remarkable contribution to the public, an Annual Award was instituted in his name in 1992.

The Khuda Bakhsh Award carries Rs.1, 00,000 and a Citation. It is conferred upon the scholars for their life-time achievements in the fields specified by the Library. So far, eight awards have been conferred upon scholars for their contribution in the respective fields. These are:

- Dr. B. N. Pande - Composite Culture of India
- Dr. Anwar Jamal Kidwai - National Integration
- Mrs. Subhadra Joshi - Composite Culture of India
- Professor Nazir Ahmad - Persian Language & Literature
- Professor S. A. H. Abidi - Persian Language & Literature
- Professor Irfan Habib - Indian History & Culture
- Professor Jagtar Singh Grewal - Sufism
- Professor Abdul Haleem Nadvi - Arabic Language & Literature

These awards were conferred by the President of India at the Rashtrapati Bhawan, New Delhi and Raj Bhawan, Patna.

The Library encourages scholars and other stakeholders and provides them all research facilities including accommodation to facilitate their research work. The Library is also conducting a post graduate course in Librariananship and Manuscriptology to produce well versed personals who can manage an oriental library effectively.[34]

The total collection of printed books and manuscripts is approximately 2, 50,000 and 21,000 respectively. The language wise break up of printed books and manuscripts is represented in the following proportion:

S. No.	*Language*	*Number of Printed Documents*	*Number of Manuscripts*
1.	Urdu	1,00,000	2113
2.	Arabic	17,000	5221
3.	Persian	17,500	6935
4.	Hindi	30,000	----
5.	English	60,000	70
6.	Sanskrit	51	85
7.	Punjabi	------	04
8.	Bhasha and Deccani	------	06
9.	Palm Leaf	-------	600
	Total Collection	**2,50,000**	**21,000**

Library of Tibetan Works and Archives, Dharamshala

13. Library of Tibetan Works and Archives, Dharamshala

Profile of the Library

The Library of Tibetan Works and Archives, Dharamshala was established in 1970 by XIV Dalai Lama and officially its door open to public in the year 1971. The Library is a home to one of only two Tibetan Oral History Projects in the World. It was founded with the aim of preserving and propagating the rich culture of Tibet to counter the massive destruction it had suffered after the Chinese invasion of Tibet in 1959 and the subsequent chaos of the Cultural Revolution.

The primary objectives of the LTWA have to provide a comprehensive Cultural Resource Centre and to promote an environment that encourages research and an exchange of knowledge between scholars and students. These factors are of the utmost importance in a contemporary world shaped by political and spiritual confusion. In trying to fulfil its objectives, the Institute's priorities include:

- Acquiring and conserving Tibetan manuscripts, books, artefacts and works of art.
- Providing access to books, manuscripts and reference works (in Tibetan as well as in foreign languages) in study areas within the Library.
- Compiling bibliographies and documentation of Library holdings and related literature available worldwide.

- Providing copies and prints of Library holdings and acting as a reference centre for such source materials.
- Publishing books and manuscripts under the Library imprint.
- Supporting research and study of the Tibetan language, both classical and modern.

The Library houses more or less 1, 09,881 manuscripts and documents in Tibetan. The Library also preserves over 13,000 printed volumes dealing with Language,Philosophy,Art and Culture, Medicine, Geography, Travel, History and Politics of Tibet and the Himalayan region. These materials are primarily in English but include some in major European and Indian languages, as well as Japanese, Chinese, Russian, and Mongolian. In the Audio and Video Collection, the Library contains more than 26,500 hours of sounds and video recording with 6,000 images of Tibet. The Museum attached with the Library contains 1, 000 artefacts and 600 statues and Thangka paintings.[35]

Publications

The Library has a separate section which deals with the publication work. Cultural Research and Publication Department publish and distribute a wide range of titles concerning Tibetan Studies. Around 200 books have been published since 1972. Apart from this, the Library also publishes two journals entitled 'Tam Tsog' and 'the Science Journal'. Both are in Tibetan language. The Publication Division publishes more than 300 titles in English language concerning Buddhist Philosophy and other aspects of Tibetan Culture. A scholarly journal entitled 'The Tibet Journal' also brings out by the Publication Division.

Renowned Manuscripts

One of the main features of the Library is its valuable manuscripts collection. The Tibetan manuscripts collection maintains more than 1,09,881 manuscripts, xylographs, documents, illuminated manuscripts and microfilm records. The Tibetan manuscripts collection is in the process of completing a general catalogue of all material in the collection.[36]

The Library started collaborating with the National Mission for Manuscripts as an MRC since September, 2003. The survey in the state of Himachal Pradesh has so far generated out 95,628 data on manuscripts and manuscript collections related to Buddhist Studies, *Vastu*, *Sangita*, *Darshana*, *Chandas*, etc. Covering **five (05) districts** with the team of four scholars and one official the MRC, the MRC has surveyed and documented **22** institutes in Himachal Pradesh. All the above mentioned data has been converted into electronic format. The Institute has conducted twenty five (25) outreach campaigns in which more than one hundred and twenty five (125) people participated. The following manuscript of the Library is included in 'Vijnannidhi' Manuscripts Treasures of India:

1. **Aryabhadra-kalapika-nama-mahayana-sutra.**

The following manuscripts are considered as very important texts in the possession of the Library:

Phags pa rigs sngags kyi rgyal po sgron ma mchog gi gzungs: Written by Bcom Idan Das in Tibetan lanuguage and available in good condition. It is a paper manuscript and complete from begining to end. The subject of the text is Tantra and contains 97-105 folios.

Don chog zin bris la: It is a complete manuscript along with very good condition on the subject of Stotra. Written in Tibetan and contains two folios, basically it is a paper manuscript.

Phags pa hu mang po bton pa zhes bya bai gzungs: Written by Bcom Idan Das in Tibetan language and contains topics on the subject of Tantra. It is a complete paper manuscript from begining to end and contains 164 folios.

Smon lam stobs po che'am kun bzang smon lam bzhugs so: It is also a paper manuscript and contains ideas and perceptions of Stotra. Written in Tibetan and complete from beginning to end and contains five folios.

Gter srung ihan thabs: It is also a paper manuscript written by Zla Ming pa in Tibetan language. Deals with Stotra and contains one folio. It is available in full from beginning to end.

Apart from the above mentioned texts, following is a list of certain other important manuscripts in its possession:

- Zhi khro phur gsum dbang sogs kyi yig chung bzhugs

- Gung drung spyod pa'i phreng ba bzhugs so
- Lam lha'i sde tshog bskul
- Lhod rgyud 'debs yid bzhin nor bu bzhugs so
- Rgyun gyi brten gtor mnga' gsol bzhugs
- bso dgung sngon 'di yi yang ma yang steng na
- Yang zab nam mka' mdzod chen las
- Bsnyan brgyud a gsal 'phrul gyis grol ma bzhugs
- Rig pa khu byug gis 'grel pa bzhugs pa'i dbu lags so
- Cog bzhugs gis sa gcod bzhugs pa'i dbu phyogs lags so
- Rgyun thag gzhung gcod dang 'grel ba bcas pa bzhugs so
- Sems lung gis rgyun bzhugs pa'i dbu phyogs lags so
- Ngo sprod ye shes mdzub tshugs
- Rgyun gyi brten gtor mnga' gsol bzhugs
- Man ngag bon sku gcer mthong
- Sems kyis ngang thag 'thud kyi gcod bzhugs so
- Sngags byang gi
- Thugs dam rgyun gyi rtsa gsum chos srung gsol mchod
- Rdzogs chen sde bcu bzhugs pa legs so
- Man ngag rig pa don 'dus
- Man ngag don gyi ga dar
- Man ngag kun 'dus mthong grol
- Man ngag ngo sprod thig 'debs
- Rig 'dzin srog sgrub las bla sgrub gsol 'debs bzhugs so
- Thugs kyi brnag pja'i skor bzhugs pa legs so
- Sngags byang gi.

Two flios of mss. Aryathadra-Kalapika-Nama-Mahayana, LTWA, Dharamshala(courtesy: NAMAMI)

Automation

The Library-cum-Archives has a specialized collection of primary and secondary documents and rare manuscripts pertaining to research and higher studies in Tibetan language, literature and culture. The Institution within a very short span provides a beautiful website, which contains almost all relevant and up-to-date information about its collection, manuscripts preservation, oral history programmes, online courses as well as calendar of events for benefit of scholars, students and other stakeholders. The website is full of images and information relevant to Tibetan language, literature and culture. Though, Online Public Access Catalogue (OPAC) of holdings of the Institution has not been displayed yet.

The manuscripts of this Organisation can be viewed on the website of National Mission for Manuscripts (NAMAMI) using its Database icon.

Digitization

It is one of the selected nodal centres by National Mission for Manuscripts as MRC. The MoU in this connection has been signed between the Library and the Mission in September, 2003. The Survey in this area has so far generated 84, 781 data on manuscripts. The Institute has conducted 25 outreach campaigns which were well received by the participants. The MRC has covered ten (10) private collections and thirty one (31) institutions covering four (4) districts. The events organized by the MRC have been broadcast in radio and local television channels, for wider propagation.[37]

In 2003, the LTWA embarked upon yet another important preservation project: The digitization of the Narthang edition of the Kangyur and Tengyur, one of the oldest and rarest manuscripts in the Library.

At present, the Institute has over fifty (50) films of 16mm in its Archive shot in seventies (70s) and eighties (80s), capturing the Tibetan life in exile during the period under consideration. These films have some of the rare footage of the early life in exile and digitalizing them will make the valuable footages available to a wider audience and will enrich the collection of that period. Due to lack of financial resources, the Library has not been able to digitize them so far, but with this grant, the Institution would be able to digitize the much necessary rare footages captured in these old films. People from all walks of life and from many different countries, including Tibetans, are increasingly making use of LTWA collections.

Other Activities

The Library is also providing assistance to the scholars and students who want to pursue higher studies concerned with Tibetan Culture and Language. For this purpose, the Library has a sepearate Research and Translation Division. An important new project for the LTWA is the launch of Central Archives of the works of his holiness the 14th Dalai Lama. The purpose of which is to collect all materials concerning his holiness Dalai Lama's teachings, writings and speeches.

The Museum, located on the first floor of the Library, originated as a repository of art and artefacts offered to his holiness the Dalai Lama. It was laid out in consultation with the National Museum of India and opened to the public in 1974.

The Museum has expanded steadily since those early days and now exhibits one of the most important collections of Tibetan art in the world. Major exhibits include a three-dimensional carved wooden Mandala of Avalokiteshvara and a thread-cross Mandala of Arya Tara, both commissioned by the LTWA; a bronze statue of Avalokiteshvara commissioned by the 13th Dalai Lama, said to stand as tall as he did; and a contemporary life-size statue of Je Tsongkhapa.

The Library possesses a collection of more than 13,000 printed books and 1, 09,881 manuscripts pertaining to Tibetan language, literature and culture. The accurate number of language wise break up of printed books and manuscripts is not available on its website or in generally available printed books.

14. Maulana Abul Kalam Azad Arabic and Persian Research Institute, Tonk

Maulana Abul Kalam Azad Arabic and Persian Research Institute, Tonk

The beautiful and impressive building of Maulana Abul Kalam Azad Arabic and Persian Research Institute, Rajasthan is located in the valley of two historical hills of Rasiya and Annapurna and is situated at city of Tonk in the state of Rajasthan in India. It is 100 kilometres southwards from

Jaipur, the capital of the Rajasthan. This Institute was established by the government of Rajasthan and has earned international repute due to its aims, objectives and achievements. A repository of knowledge, the Institute has a collection of 8,513 manuscripts, 31,452 printed books, 719 Faramin (letters), 17,701 old magazines and 65,000 judgement files of the Shariat Records (Islamic Ethical Codes) of the erstwhile Tonk State in addition to the historical documents belonging to the old Munshi Khana Huzuri of the same state. This literary treasure of Arabic and Persian as well as Urdu belongs to the 5th century of the Hijra and onwards. It consists of the original works including edited and translated manuscripts and publications on the subjects relating to Holy Quran, Hadees (Words, Works and Acceptance of Prophet Muhammad,pbuh), Fiqh (Islamic Jurisprudence), Tasawwuf (Islamic Mysticism), Philosophy, Seerat (Traditions of the Prophet Muhammad, pbuh), History, Medicines, Astrology, Literature and Malfuzat (writings) of the holy saints with Asnad, Tughrajat and the exhibits of decorative Calligraphic Art.

This invaluable literary collection owes its initial establishment to Yameen-ud-Daulah Wazir-ul-Mulk, Nawab Muhammad 'Ali Khan, the third ruler of erstwhile Tonk State in the year 1867. Saeed-ud-Daulah, the late Nawab Saadat Ali Khan had transferred it to the newly established Saeediyah Library Building in the year 1946, which was known as District Library at that time. A number of manuscripts and printed documents written in Arabic and Persian had been transferred to the Institute from 1961 to 1978 available in the state of Rajasthan. During Maulana Azad Centenary Celebrations in 1989, this Institute renamed as Maulana Abul Kalam Azad Arabic and Persian Research Institute Rajasthan, Tonk.

The Institute preserves many collections by the name of the donor such as Maulana Shaghil Collection, Jaipur; Jauhar Collection, Tonk; Pundit Ram Niwas Nadeem Collection, Tonk; Maulana Ubaid Arab Collection, Bhopal; Hafiz Qamar Asif Collection, Ajmer; Chand Bihari Lal 'Saba' Collection, Jaipur, Maulawi Hakim Muhammad Ahmad Collection, Tonk, Capt.

Sahibzadah M. Shamsher Khan 'Shaaheen' Collection, Tonk, Mufti Akhter Hussain Collection, Kota and Manzoor Alam Collection, Tonk etc.

The main objectives of the Institute are as follows:

- To acquire, preserve and conserve Arabic and Persian original sources of historical and cultural importance available in Rajasthan or pertaining to Rajasthan.
- To promote and cultivate Arabic and Persian research and studies based primarily on the above mentioned sources and to provide facilities and amenities to scholars.
- To edit, translate, publish and decipher original sources.
- To commission competent scholars to facilitate editing, deciphering, translating etc. of original sources and to undertake work on various aspects related to the objectives of the Institute.
- To facilitate and assist in the documentation of Arabic and Persian source material of research value available with bodies other than the Institute.
- To encourage, facilitate and to establish techniques of research methodology in Arabic and Persian studies.
- To undertake and encourage the study of the declining oriental arts like calligraphy and palaeography etc.
- To Institute provides prizes, scholarships, fellowships and awards for research and higher studies in Orientology.
- To undertake all necessary measures to promote and advance the aims and objects of the Institute e.g. to organize seminars, symposia, colloquia, conferences, workshops, exhibitions and extension lectures etc. and publication of research Journals.

Publications

Since its inception, the Institute has been publishing books, descriptive catalogues and certain translated works on a range of themes. Till date, the Institute has published a total of eighty eight (88) publication including six (6) English catalogues, six (6) Urdu catalogues, twenty six (26) reference journals, eighteen n(18) translation works and thirty two (32) other publications. Following is the list of descriptive catalogues being published by the Institute till date:

1. Catalogue of the Arabic manuscripts: Volume I (English), 1980.
2. Catalogue of the Arabic manuscripts: Volume II (English), 1983.
3. Catalogue of the Arabic manuscripts: Volume III (English), 1991.
4. Descriptive Catalogue of the Persian manuscripts of History: Volume I (English), 1987.
5. Descriptive Catalogue of the Persian manuscripts of History: Volume II (English), 1996.
6. Descriptive Catalogue of the Persian manuscripts of History: Volume III (English), 2006.
7. Khazinat ul Makhtutat: Volume I (Urdu), 1981.
8. Khazinat ul Makhtutat: Volume II (Urdu), 1983.
9. Khazinat ul Makhtutat: Volume III (Urdu), 1984.
10. Khazinat ul Makhtutat: Volume IV (Urdu), 1998-99.
11. Khazinat ul Makhtutat : Volume V (Part–I), (Urdu), 2001-
12. Khazinat ul-Makhtutat, Volume V (Part II), (Urdu), 2008.

Apart from the above mentioned descriptive catalogues, the Institute has also published a number of translation works on various themes which include.

1. Tarikh-i-Qila-i-Ranthambhore (Urdu), 1987.
2. Contribution of Non-Muslims towards Persian Literature in Rajasthan (Hindi), 1988.
3. Qasr-i-Ilm (Hindi), 1989
4. Risalah Itriyat (Urdu), 1991.
5. Rubaiyat-i-Sarmad (Urdu), 1991.
6. Chahar Gulshan (Hindi), 1991.
7. Khattati (Tazkira-i-Khushnawisan) (Urdu) 1995

8. Kitabush-Shatranj (Urdu), 1996.
9. Mujamul Musannifin (Urdu), Vol. III 1997.
10. Mujamul Musannifin (Urdu) Vol. IV, 2006.
11. Tarikh-i-Tonk (Hindi), 1997.
12. Aina-i-Ayyam (Urdu), 1997-98.
13. Mirat-i-Aftab Numa Vol.I (Urdu) 2001
14. Tahqiqul Auzan (Urdu), 2001.
15. Mirat-i Aftab Numa Vol II, (Urdu), 2004
16. Mirat-i Aftab Numa Vol III, (Urdu), 2005
17. Amir Namah (Hindi), 2003
18. Talqih-i-Fuhum-i-Ahlil Asar, 2010
19. Historical Heritage (English) 1980
20. Qasr-i-Ilm (Urdu), 1980.
21. Islami Hind men Fann-i-Khattati (Urdu), 1980.
22. Tonk ki Mahanta ke do Minar (Hindi), 1980.
23. Hazrat Ameer Khusroo aur Tonk (Urdu), 1981.
24. Kalam-i-Saib Vol. I (Persian), 1982
25. Contribution of Non-Muslims towards Persian Literature in Rajasthan (Urdu), 1984.
26. Maqasid-ul-Arifin (Persian), 1984.
27. Contribution of Non-Muslims towards Urdu Literature in Rajasthan (Urdu), 1985.
28. Tazkirah-i-Sufia-i-Delhi(Zikr-i-Jamee-i-Aulia-i-Delhi) (Persian), 1987
29. Ad-Dibajah Ala Ibn-i-Majah (Arabic), 1990
30. Dar-us-Suroor Jaipur (Arabic), 1995
31. Anwar-i-Ilm-w-Irfan (Urdu) Vol. I, 1997-98.
32. Tarikh-i-Tonk (Urdu), 1999
33. Hayat Haider Hasan Khan Tonki (Arabic) 1999.
34. Fatawa Adalat-i-Shara Sharif Tonk (Kitab-ut-Talaq, Volume I), (Urdu), 2002.
35. Fatawa Adalat-i-Shara Sharif Tonk (Kitab-ut-Talaq, Volume. II), (Urdu), 2005.

36. Fatawa Adalat-i-Shara Sharif Tonk (Kitab-ut-Talaq, Volume III), (Urdu), 2006.
37. Tazkirah -e - Ulama-e– Tonk, Volume I, (Urdu), 2006.
38. Mashriqi Rajputana ke Qadim Adabi Marakiz (Alwar, Bharatpur Aur Dholpur), (Urdu), 2006.
39. Fatawa Adalat-i-Shara Sharif Tonk Kitab-ul-Faraiz (Wirasat) Vol. I, (Urdu), 2008.
40. Rajasthan Ki Adabi Taareekh ke Chand Urdu Marakiz, (Urdu), 2008.
41. Arabic Persian Research Institute, Tonk (English), 2008
42. Souvenir-2004
43. Al-Lualiul Muziyyah Fi Hilyati Khairil Bariyyah, Volume I, (Persian), 2009.
44. Fatawa Adalat-i-Shara Sharif Tonk (Kitab-ut-Talaq, volume IV), (Urdu) -2009.
45. Tonk ke Hukmaran-i-Zeeshan (Tehzib-o-Saqafat), volume I (Urdu), 2009.
46. Kalam-i-Bismil, 2010, (Hindi).
47. Tonk Ke Hukmaran-i-Zeeshan, volume II, 2010, (Urdu).
48. Futuhul Islam, Vol. I, (Urdu), 2010.
49. Dastan Aba Gulshan-i-Ishq (Urdu), 2010
50. Souvenir-2010.

Renowned Manuscripts

This Institute is well known to the world for its rare manuscripts on Historiography, Orientology, Islamic Studies, Sufism, Urdu, Arabic and Persian Literature, Catalogues, Medicines, Auto-biographies, Medieval History, Literature based on Independence, Calligraphy, Philosophy, and Calligraphic Art etc. The manuscripts are decorated with gold and lapis lazuli work and many of them are the best specimens of calligraphy. There are some Tughras of beautiful calligraphic designs also preserves in its Library. Apart from Arabic and Persian manuscripts, there are a good number of rare manuscripts of Urdu on various subjects pertaining to 19th Century preserved here. Most of the manuscripts are specifically related to Rajasthan not generally available in other libraries of the Country.

Details about a few very important manuscripts of this Library are as follows:

Si Warqai Quran Majid: A masterpiece of illumination and artistic beauty which exhibits a superb calligraphic art of Mughal era. The whole manuscript comprises only thirty folios with the striking feature of having been transcribed each line with the letter 'Alif' in red with double Jadwal and interlinear space in gold. Its binding is an elegant specimen of Persian lacquer work.

This copy is attributed to the calligraphy of Abul Baqi who had been awarded the title of Yaqut Raqam and weighed against the currency as a reward of the work by the Mughal king Shahjahan.

Alamgiri Quran Majid: One more exceptional specimen of calligraphy with an imaginative, floral and decorated work and illumination of Mughal era manuscript is worth mentioning. The second and the third page contain Lawh in gold. On the margin artistic floral designs are demonstrated in gold with important glosses and notes. It appears that this codex had a long time ago been housed in the library of great Mughals. On its first page is an endorsement in Persian which runs as under 'from the library of Mirza Muhammad Humayun Shah Bahadur, the son of Mirza Muhammad Kam Bakhsh Alam Bahadur'. Though, it is incomplete but very unique due to above mentioned features and written in Naskh.

At-Talkhis: This manuscript is an ostensibly rare, antique and authentic commentary of the holy Quran composed by Abul Abbas Ahmad Yusuf-al-Kawashi in 649 A.H. / 1251 A.D. No copy of this text has been traced out so for. It is condensed from three commentaries viz Tafsir-ut-Tam, Tafsir-ul-Hasan and Tafsir-ul-Kai, as observed by Haji Khalifah in his 'Kashf-uz-Zunun'.

The authencity and the rarity of this manuscript are enhanced as it was collated from the original manuscript of the commentator and subsequently compared with the manuscript which had been transcribed by the commentator himself. It was copied during the Commentator's life time in 677 A.H. /1278 A.D. by the calligrapher Abd-al-Qahir bin Mahmud bin Abu Bakr, a prolific writer and eminent scholar who had been a pupil of the Commentator.

Aaraz-us-Siyasah: It is an exceedingly rare and unique text on history and politics of Persia. It throws a deluge of light on the history, civics, politics and culture of Persia extending right from Jamshid Malik upto Sultan Sanjar bin Malik (1092 A.H. /1681 A.D. to 1157 A.H. /1744 A.D.). The name of each king is written in red colour. Before commencing with the history of of the Persian emperors, the author has given the tables of all the kings and then the account of each king has been confined to some folios dealing with the moral dictums and maxims of the kings and caliphs along with a treatment of social and cultural life of the people of that era. It is divided into chapters, and further, sub divided into various sections.

The pattern of Nastaliq and the calligraphic characteristics of the Persian alphabet and the other ligatures and strokes coupled with the Persian paper and the unfaded ink used, amply establish the fact that the manuscript had been written in the life time of the author. It is also supposed to be the transcript of the author himself. All the artistic signs and calligraphic features of the early 18th century A.D. are profusely visible throughout the text.

Iqbal Nama-i-Jahhangiri: Iqbal Nama often called, Jahangir Namah, was completed in Kashmir in 1029 A.H. / 1619-20 A.D. corresponding to the fifteenth regnal year of Jahangir, but it was supplemented by the author till the death of Jahangir. It comprise three volumes, the first two of which contain the history of Babur, Humayun and Akbar and are rare according to Rieu extremely rare while the third devoted to reign of Jahangir, is very common.

Its author Muhammad Sharif who is distinguished from Sharif Khan, the Amir-ul-Umara in the early reign of Jahangir, was born in an undistinguished family of Persia, but due to his handsome fortunes and meritorious service he was awarded a military command (mansab) and the title of Mutamad Khan, in the third regnal year of Jahangir. This Institute contains a number of copies of this text.

Shahjahan Namah Manzum: A rare and perhaps the original work versified by Abu Talib Kalim Hamadani, a contemporary poet-laureate, commencing with hilayah-i-Shahjahan (external features and vitues), his geneology, his campaigns, and enterprises and other related historical events of his father's reign. The military campaigns to Kabul, Qandhar, the Deccan and Gujarat and the capture of Kangra-Hugli are especially described.

The manuscript comprises two parts bound in one. The first part contains events of Jahangir's reign related to prince Khurram (Shahjahan) ending at folios number 57 and the second part ends abruptly at folio number 160, describing the military campaigns of Shahjahan launched under the generalship of his third son Shuja. From a colophonic note it is supposed to have been copied either in 1042 A.H. /1632 A.D. or 1142 A.h. /1729 A.D., as only the last two digits are given but from calligraphy, it appears that it might have been transcribed in 1042 A.H. /1632 A.D.

Humayun Namah: Compiled by Ghiyas-ud-Din bin Humam-ud-Din known as Khawand Amir (died after 941 A.H. /1534 A.D.) and was copied by Muhammad Husain in 1302 A.H. /1884 A.D. It is an account of rules, ordinances, daily programmes and other customs, practices and inventions of the king Humayun and also of some buildings eracted by him. This is the last celebrated work of the reputed historian a short time before his demise.

Amir Namah: A rare and unpublished Persian manuscript authored by Munshi Lal Shadan of Bilgram. He was private secretary to Nawab Amir Khan. Amir Namah is a life sketch of a Pathan leader Amir Khan who was born soldier, remained a soldier and died as a soldier, endowed with extraordinary military genius, a soldier's dash and a general's tactical skills. The text also throws light on the culture and cutoms of that period.

Miftah-ul-Asrar: A rare and unpublished general history by anonymous authors with special refrrence to Indian rulers brought down to the accession of Shihab-ud-din Shahjahan bin Nur-ud-Din Jahangir.

The work is divided into 12 Khizanahs, further subdivided into various Ganjinahs dealing with Islamic history, general history, the Mughal history, the Indian Timurids and the Deccan rulers.

Tarikh-i-Jahan Numa: Written by Hakim Ilahi famous with Hakim-ul-Hind, copied from the original manuscript from the author written in his own hand in 13th /19th century. It is a topographical account of the world in general derived from the English geographical and Persian historical works. It is a copy of the original transcript of the author comprising one Muqaddimah, two Maqalat and one Khatimah. Written in Nastaliq and provided with marginal notes and corrections written in his own hand as is confirmed by a note subscribed on the title page.

Kitab-ul-Gharibain: It is a rare, perhaps the oldest and authentic copy of archival importance. The work is an old lexicon of less familiar words occurring in the holy Hadees. There are a few salient features of calligraphy, antiquity, Asnaad, and marginal notes which have made it a rare asset of pre-eminence.

Its author is Abu Ubaid Ahmad bin Muhammad bin Abi Ubaid-al-Abdi-al-Harawi-al-Fashani who got himself educated by Abu Mansur al-Azhari, a reputed Arabic scholar of varying talents and tastes. He died in 401 A.H. /1011 A.D.

Shams-ul-Uloom: A rare and authentic treatise of intrinsic values, according to Haji Khalifah, comprises 18 volumes subdivided into various Kitabs. The author Nashwan bin Said bin Nashwan-al-Himyari was an accomplished scholar of etymology, syntax, lexicography, historiography, jurisprudence, and poet as well. Although, he was adept in Quranic Sciences, he had a penetrating acumen in lexicography and Arabic classics. He breathed his last in 573 A.H. / 1177 A.D.Written in Arabic and script is Yamani Naskh, the text is very important due to number of characteristics.

Tarikh-i-Ahmadi: A very and rare and unpublished history on the life and achievements of Sayyid Ahmad Shaheed, the celebrated Muslim sage and indomitable freedom fighter of 13th /19th century. Sayyid Jafar Ali bin Sayyid Qutb Ali was an accomplished scholar of Arabic and Persian. He got his education from Haider Ali Rampuri Tonki and Shah Muhammad Ishaq. He had been a staunch follower of Sayyid Sahib, after whose martyrdom, Nawab Wazir-ud-Daulah invited him to compile this historical work in Tonk. The author had been personal secretary to Sayyid Ahmad Shahid during his holy wars against the British. Its other copies are scarcely found elsewhere. The modern famous historian Ghulam Rasul Mihr has used this manuscript while compiling his biography on Sayyid Ahmad Shaheed.

Tarikh-i-Rajasthan or Nasb-ul-Ansab: Tarikh-i-Rajasthan is a rare and original work. It deals with the history of the rulers of Jaipur, Marwar, Mewar, and Hadauti dynasties with special refrence to the political affairs relating to the Punjab, the Deccan, Bengal, Gujarat and Sindh. The manuscript contains three sections called Tabaqat.

The author Kali Ram was a native of Ajmer. In his preface, he says that he undertook this work in deference to the wishes of Maharaja Sawai Pratap Singh in 1209 A.H. /1794 A.D. From the contents of this history, it appears that the author must have consulted the archives of the Jaipur State, the Pothi Khanah, Kapat Duwarah, Tawshak Khanah records comprising Farmans, Asnads, and the Akhbarat. The author might have had all the authentic records at his disposal as indicated by himself in the Preface. In the beginning, he was attached to the office of the Munshi Khanah holding the post of epistolographer. He was very fond of reading the works on History. Since the beginning of his service he had been collectionng the raw material from Persian and Hindi manuscripts and personal collections of the Rajah. The manuscript was completed in V.S. 1851 corresponding to 1209 A.H. /1794 A.D. No other copy of it is known to exist.

Other very important manuscripts in Institute's possession are:

- Tarikh-i-Gharibi (Versified)
- Diwan-e-Mirza Akbar Ali Baig 'Gul' (Poetry)
- Qissah-i-Rangeen Guftar by Azmatullah Niyaz) (Prose)
- Bairam Namah by Mohammad Umar Fasih) (Prose)
- Qurrat-ul-Uyun by Nawab Mohammad Ali Khan) (Prose)
- Diwan-i-Ishq by Shaikh Nizam-ud-Din) (Poetry)
- Tarikh-i-Mulhim by Maulana Ahtisham -ud-Din 'Shaukat') (Versified)
- Ain-ul-Ilm by Jamaluddin Muhammad-al-Balkhi
- Awariful Maarif by Shahabuddin Suharwardi
- Unwan-ush-Sharf by Maulvi Saadullah
- Qissa Qazi wa Duzd by Shah Inayatullah Alavi
- Muraqqa Shah Kalimullah Jahanabadi, Risalah Ganjul-Asrar by Shah Kalimullah Jahanabadi and Shaikh Farid Masud
- Miftah-al-Salat by Mulla Fateh Muhammad
- Mata-i-Dard by Mirza Hakim Muhammad Yahya
- Ihya-al-uloom-ud-Din by Zain-al-Din Abu Hamid Muhammad Al-Ghazzali
- Ar-Risalatul-Qushairiyah by Abul-Qasim Abdul-Karim Al-Qushairi
- Masail-al-Taalim-fi-Fiqh-us-Shafiyee by Abu Abdur-Rahman Afzal
- Pand Namah, Jahangir Badshah by Jahangir
- Tazyinul-Ibarah li-Tahsin-al-Isharah by Mulla Nooruddin Ali Bin Sultan Muhammad Al-Qari
- Asrarul-Wajud by Shah Muhammad Ikram-ud-Din Chishti
- Maasim-al-Aasim by Zuhoorul Haq Phulwari
- Tarikh-i-Firoz Shahi by Zia-ud-Din Burni.

Automation

The Institute has a beautiful and very informative website of its own which is developed and hosted by National

Informatics Centre (NIC). It contains valuable information about origin, aims, activities, publications, printed books and manuscripts of the institute in detailed manner. It is very informative in its thought content.

Digitization

The Institute has not started digitization work till date.

Other Activities

An Art Gallery is also started from 2002, in which many artistic presentations of different classes are displayed. Namda calligraphy, art of charming photography, collection of postage stamps etc. capture the eye of the visitors. Calligraphy on human hair, pulse, rice and sesame along with the lines written inside the transparent glass bottles has made the Institute a centre of attraction of tourists and visitors. A seperate hall with the name of "Display Hall" is also maintained for displaying some of the important and historical manuscripts enriched with some of the seal impressions of kings, princesses etc. and notes in their own hand writings with signatures etc., which are preserved under the intact show-cases covered with a transparent glass for the common people. The various manuscripts on different subjects written with golden frontispiece and floral designs drawn with the ink made of precious stones are a centre of attraction not only for the scholars but also for the general public.

The total number of printed books and manuscripts are 31,452 and 8,513 respectively written in various languages such as Arabic, Persian, Urdu, Hindi and English etc. Language wise break up of books and manuscripts is neither in printed books so farnor on on its website.

Maharaja Serfoji's Saraswati Mahal Library, Thanjavur

15. Maharaja Serfoji's Saraswati Mahal Library, Thanjavur

Profile of the Library

It is one of the richest libraries of India as far as manuscripts of Indian origin are concerned. It was founded in 16th century by Nayaka rulers of Thanjavur. Since 1918, the Saraswati Mahal Library has been a possession of the state of Tamil Nadu. The official name of the Library was changed to 'Thanjavur Maharaja Serfoji's Saraswati Mahal Library' in honor of the great royal Marathan patron.

Most of its collections are based on rare manuscripts and printed volumes in Sanskrit, Tamil, Marathi and Telugu languages which reflects the culture and history of South India. The Library possesses approximately 52,094 printed books, 909 bound volumes of periodicals, 47,625 manuscripts, 1, 159 photographic slides, 35 maps, 1,317 microfilm rolls, and 30 wooden paintings. It is also subscribing to 10 journals and 4 news papers.[38]

Thanjavur Maharaja Serfoji's Saraswati Mahal Library is the one among the few medieval libraries that exist in the world. The 'Encyclopedia Britannica' in its Survey of libraries of the World refers to this as the most remarkable libraries in India. The Library is considered as one of the biggest manuscript library in Asia. The Library houses a rich and rare collection of manuscripts on Art, Culture and Literature, numbering around several thousands. The manuscripts are available both in palm leaves and paper on various forms on various subjects in Tamil, Telugu, Sanskrit, and Marathi languages. The oldest palm leaf manuscript here is 'Phalavat, belonging to 11th century.the earliest paper manuscript is 'Bhamati' dated 1476 A.D. The earliest printed book in the Library is dated 1692 A.D.

Publications

One of the most vital objectives of the Library is to publish rare and unpublished manuscripts for the benefit of the scholars and general public at large. By the end of 1951, sixty seven titles were published by this Library. Number of descriptive catalogues of its holdings has already been published. The descriptive catalogue of Sanskrit Manuscripts prepared by P.P.Subramania Sastri in 19 volumes published in 1932, the Marathi Catalogue in 1932, and the Tamil catalogue in 1927.[39]

This Library also publishes books on rare manuscripts from time to time. During the year 2002-2005, it has published a total number of 38 books for first edition and 54 reprint editions.[40]

The Library has also publishing a journal for the benefit of scholars and other users and include contents about rare manuscripts of historical importance in Indology, Sanskrit, and South Indian languages and literature.[41]

Renowned Manuscripts:

The preservation of rare and exceptionally important manuscripts is one of the most important features of this Library. The Library has classified its manuscripts collection in following languages:

- Sanskrit Manuscript Collection
- Tamil Manuscripts Collection
- Telugu Manuscripts Collection
- Marathi Manuscript Collection
- Modi Manuscripts Collection and
- Rare and Illustrated Manuscripts Collection.

Among the numerous rare and illustrated manuscripts attention may be drawn to some of the rarest among the rare:

Kunda Kriti: It is a palm leaf manuscript dealing with the subject of Dharamshastra (Hindu religion). Written by Ram Chandra in Sanskirit language using Nandinagari script.

Charan Vyuh: This palm leaf manuscript written by Shaunak deals with the subject of Vedas. Written in Sanskirit language with Devanagari script.

Gita Govinda: This Gita Govinda manuscript is written by Jai Dev in Sanskirit language. Unfortunately the said manuscript is incomplete; though still a rare and valuable copy of the text on the subject. It is a palm leaf manuscript in poetical verses with Grantha script.

Sangeet Sudhaker: It is an incomplete palm leaf manuscript written in Sanskirit using Devanagari script. Deals with the subject of Indian Music and written by Hari Pal Dev.

Tarkbhasha Vyakhya: It is a palm leaf manuscript deals with the subject of Oriental and Hindu philosophy. Though, it is also an incomplete text but still very relevant treatise on the subject concerned. Authored by Gopi Nath in Sanskirit language using grantha script. Contains a total of 65 folios.

Tarkbhasha Prakash: The manuscript is written by Govardhan in Sanskirit language. It is a palm leaf manuscript and Telugu script has been used for writing the text. Contains 67 folios and the subject of the text is Oriental and Hindu philiosophy.

Apart from the above mentioned rare manuscripts, the following texts are also very important in the collection of the Library:

Bhamati:A paper manuscript written 1468 in Benaras

- Bhagavata Gita (smallest pocket size)
- Bhagavata Gita: A commentary written by a Muslim poet Ambar Hussain in Marathi
- Chitra Ramayana
- Maha Bharata Tatparyanirray Vyakhya by Shri Niwas

- Bhagavata Bhakti Nirray by Ananta Dev
- Kirtan by Ambi Shastri
- Maha Bharata Tatparyanirray Vyakhya by Varad Raj
- Jnanan Pradeepika by Chandra Shekhar
- Sangeet Muktawali by Devender
- Ghazini Mohammad: A pictorial representation.

A folio from a mss. MSSML, Thanjavur (courtesy: NAMAMI)

Automation

Computerization/Automation is one of the most fundamental tasks of any institution in the Internet era. TMSSM Library is no exception to this segment. The Computer Centre of the Library was established in year 1977. It was equipped with one multimedia, one DTP and 5 nodes, two dot matrix printers, one laser printer and one desk scanner were bought at first phase. The Library has installed many computers in 1998 for the computerisation of Library activities. As a first phase, the library catalogues are being stored in the computer system for easy information retrieval. Computerized cataloguing System for manuscripts and books being implemented. The Library has developed its own website with help of NIC Centre, Chennai in 1998.[42]

The information regarding its manuscripts may be seen on the manuscripts database created by National Mission for Manuscripts (NAMAMI) through Mission's website.

Digitization

The Institution has been selected by National Mission for Manuscripts for surveying, documentation, awareness and training in manuscript preservation and providing assistance to manuscript perseveres of the Institution and individuals possessing manuscripts. The Library has collected data for more than 500 manuscripts and conducted a workshop on preventive conservation of Palm Leaf Manuscripts. The Library also celebrated Manuscript Day with an Awareness Programme and Exhibition on 31 January 2005.

The MRC and MCC of National Mission for Manuscripts at Maharaja Serfoji's Saraswati Mahal Library, Thanjavur have been functioning since September, 2003 and October, 2003 respectively. The MRC has so far prepared 35,914 electronic data of manuscripts in Tamil Nadu. It has covered 34 collections covering 2 districts during survey and has held 2 publicity campaigns. The MCC has so far taken preventive care of 494 manuscripts and given curative conservation treatment to 427 manuscripts.

The Library employs several indigenous methods of conservation and manuscript storage. This MCC in collaboration with Tamil Nadu Government Museum has conducted 2workshops and publicity programmes. The MCC has conducted preventive conservation activities on both palm leaf and paper manuscripts covering ten (10) institutions.[43]

Other Activities

Apart from the preservation of rare and important documents in major oriental languages, the Library also maintains a good museum in which valuable manuscripts, paintings, artifacts, drawings etc are preserved.[44]

The Library is preparing a list of institutions, mutts and individuals in possession of manuscripts in Tamil language in support of the National Mission for preservation of manuscripts projects of Government of India. A monthly literary programme is conducted; and eminent literary scholar delivers lectures every month. This is aimed to interact with the public and to develop library consciousness among them.

The Library has also conducted various training courses in the past few years according to following mentioned schedules.

- Three weeks training course on Tamil Manuscriptology from 4.3.2004 to 25.3.2004
- Three days Workshop on Conservation of Library materials from 12.03.2004 to 14.03.2004.
- Three weeks course on Grantha Script from 25-3-2004 to 18-4-2004
- Three days Workshop on Conservation of Library materials from 20.03.2006 to 22.03.2006.[45]

The language wise break up of printed books and manuscripts in major oriental languages are as follows:

S. No.	*Language*	*Number of Printed Books*	*Number of Manuscripts*
1.	Sanskrit	------	39,300
2.	Tamil	------	3,780
3.	Telugu	-------	846
4.	Marathi	------	3,076
5.	Hindi	-------	100
6.	Urdu and Persian	-------	22
5.	Modi Documents(Marathi Raj Records)	------	1,342 bundles
	Total Collection	**52,094**	**47,625**

16. National Library of India, Kolkata

National Library of India, Kolkata

Profile of the Library

The National Library, Kolkata is biggest library in the Indian Subcontinent. It is an organization of importance for the whole of the Nation. The National Library situated at Kolkata is the national Library of India after India got freedom in 1947. It was established under the patronage of 'Department of Culture 'Ministry of Tourism and Culture, Government of India. It is a depository Library; therefore it receives books in almost all languages of India including Urdu, Arabic, Persian, Telugu, Tamil, and Hindi etc.

The basic aims of the Library include:

- Acquisition and conservation of all national and significant productions of printed material, excluding ephemera.
- Collection of printed documents concerning with the Nation or about the Nation
- Acquisition of foreign documents required by the Country
- Rendering of bibliographical and document services of current and retrospective material, and

- Acting as a referral centre purveying accurate and full knowledge.[46]

National Library was established in 1948 with the passing of the Imperial Library Act, 1948. The Library has the status of an Institution of National Importance. It is engaged in the task of acquisition and conservation of all significant production of printed material. The Library also undertakes the conservation of manuscripts of national importance. It acts as a referral center purveying full and accurate knowledge of all sources of bibliographical information and participation in international bibliographical activities. It has a rich collection of Persian, Sanskrit, Arabic and Tamil manuscripts and also rare printed books. It is one of the recipient library under the Delivery of Books and Newspapers (Public Libraries) Act, 1954 and the repository library in South Asia. It is also a repository of the United Nations publications as well as official documents of selected foreign countries.

One of the most important features of this Library is its collection of extremely singular documents and thus, the Library has a separate section for rare books. Earlier, these items were stacked with other books. But, in 1973, a separate rare books division was set up to take care of these important books. At present the books published prior to 1860 are considered as rare books. Along with such materials, manuscripts and microfilms of the Library also stacked in this division. The division also provides reading facilities to the users who wish to consult these items. At present the division has 4,700 monographs, 3,227 manuscripts and 1,500 microfilms. The oldest book of the library is in Latin language. Palm leaves manuscript is also preserved in this division.

Some valuable personal collections like Sir Asutosh Mukhopadhyay Collection, Prof. Vaiyapuri Pillai Collection, and Sir Jadunath Sarkar Collection etc. have been gifted here. Besides these, a good number of selected documents from various disciplines written in English are purchased every year. The Library also holds a considerable number of electronic documents which are received through the above mentioned act, through purchase, while some are generated by scanning of old brittle documents in the Library itself. The National Library has elaborate arrangements for physical conservation of books for posterity.

Publications

The Library is publishing a newsletter "NL Newsletter" regularly to make inform the public about its activities and events.

Apart from the newsletter, the Library has published many descriptive and bibliographic catalogues of its rare books and manuscripts.

Renowned Manuscripts

The National Library preserves about 3,227 rare and historically very important manuscripts in a variety of languages. There is a rich collection of Arabic and Persian manuscripts from Buhar in the district of Burdwan; manuscripts of Sir Jadunath Sarkar and his correspondence with Dr. G.S. Sardesai, Sanskrit manuscripts from Rewa Estate and of Dr. Thibant and Dr. Ram Das Sen; ancient Tamil palm leaf manuscripts on Vaiyapuri Pillai collection; personal papers of Sir Tej Bahadur Sapru, B.S. Moonjee and Hari Nath De; diaries of Satya Kinkar Sahara; manuscripts from poet Jibanananda Das and Bishnu Dey; fragments of Bibhuti Bhusan Bandopadhyay's manuscript of Pather Panchali; paper clippings of H.K.Ghosh ; and many other collections. These manuscripts, diaries and press clippings are preserved along with rare books in the Rare Books Division. The xylograph presented by H.E., the Dalai Lama is also available in this collection.

Recently, the Library has received the personal correspondence of Netaji Subash Chandra Bose and his illustrious brother Sarat Chandra Bose; and even more recently, the Bengali manuscripts of famous poet Kabisekher Kalidas Roy and the personal diaries and correspondence of Sir Jadu Nath Sarkar.

Among the valuable rare books and manuscripts, mention may be made of some of the prize possessions:

Mirat-i-Jahan Numa: A correct and old copy of the Mirat-i-Jahan Numa or general history of the World, compiled under Aurangzeb before 1094 A.H. / 1682 A.D. It is an enlarged recension of the Mirat-ul-Aalam which is due, like the shorter work, to the authoeship of Muhammad Baqa and not to Bakhtawar Khan. It was edited after author's death by his sister's son Muhammad Shafi in 1095 A.H./1683 A.D., regarding which question see the Bankipur Library catalogue number 477.

Written in good Nastaliq within red ruled borders. The date of transcription in the Colophon is hopelessly damaged, but the name of the scribe, as far as the mutilation allows us to decipher it, reads as Abd-un-Nabi Syed Firoz Saharanpuri.

Futuh-i-ibn Aasam: A Persian translation of Khwaja Abu Muhammad Ahmad bin Aasam-al-Kufi's Arabic work 'Futuh' or history of the Islam from Prophet Muhammad's (PBUH) death to the death of Hasan (R.A.) and Husayn (R.A.) and accession of Yezid in 680 A.H.

The translation was undertaken about 596 A.H. /1199 A.D. by Muhammad bin Ahmad-al-Mustaufi-al-Harawi who died after finishing only a small portion of the work. It was continued and completed by Muhammad bin Ahmad bin Abi Bakr-al-Katib-al-Mabarnabadi.

Written in clear Nastaliq within gold and coloured rule borders, with a front space and an illuminated Unwan (Title).

Zafar Namah: The well known history of emperor Timur from his birth to his death, written by Sharf-ud-Din-al-Yazdi, who completed it, according to Habib-us-Siyar in 828 A.H. / 1424 A.D.

The work has been published in the Bibliotheca Indica series at Calcutta in 1887. Written in clear Nastaliq with the headings in red. The first and the last folios are damaged. Several folios at the beginning have been supplied at a later stage.

Mafatih-al-Ajam: A rare copy of the history of the ancient Persian dynasties and their kings, written by the order of the celebrated Wazir Mir Ali Shir, by Abul Hasan Tabari. The first three folios supplied in a later hand, are hopelessly damaged.

The Author divided the work into four Tabaqat (Sections), devoted to four ancient dynasties of the Persia, the Pishadians, the Kayanians, the Ashkanians and the Sasanians. Written in good Nastaliq with rubics. Not dated, apparently a work of 17th Century A.D.

Tarikh-i-Herat: This unique and exceedingly valuable work of which no other copy seems to be extent, is no doubt the most valuable possession of the this Library. It gives, an elaborate scale, an accurate account of the city of Herat and the Malik kings of Kurt race who ruled there, and treats of all the important events of historical interst which took place there between the years 618-721 A.H. /1221-1321 A.D. Moin Asafzai, the author of the Raudat-al-Jannat (a popular history of Herat), who quotes this work as one of his sources, not only freely borrows from it, but bases his entire account of the aforesaid period exclusively on it.

The author who calls himself in the Preface Sayf ibn Muhammad bin Yaqub-al-Harawi but later on simply Sayfi, says that after composing the the ethical work Majmuah-i-Ghiyasi, which he dedicated to his partron Malik Ghiyas-ud-Din Kurt, the fourth king of the Herat of the Kurt race, who reigned from 708-729 A.H. /1308-1328 A.D., he was ordered by the said king to write a history of the events which took place in Herat after Chingiz Khan's death down to his time.

Written in a beautiful gold and clear Naskh on good thick paper with the headings in red throughout the copy. The manuscript is not dated, but the nature of the handwriting and the general appearance of the copy tend to suggest that it was transcribed during the lifetime of the author or immediately after his death. The manuscript is worm eaten, mutilated and loosened from the original binding, but fortunately no foliuos seems to be missing.

Tarikh-i-Masudi: A very splendid copy of the well known history of the reign of Sultan Masud bin Sultan Subuktgin, from 421-432 A.H. / 1030-1040 A.D. by Abul Fadl Muhammad bin Husayn-al-Bayhaqi, who died in 470 A.H. /1077 A.D.

The work is also known as Tarikh-i-Beyhaqi, has been printed in the Bibliotheca Indica, Calcutta in 1862. Written in beautiful Nastaliq, within gold ruled borders, with a finely illuminated front space and a double page Unwan (Title). There are several gaps in the present text.

Bayan-i- Waqi: A history of Nadir Shah from his invasion of India down to his death in 1160 A.H. /1747 A.D. and of the events that took place during the reigns of Muhammad Shah and Ahmad Shah, together with a narrative of the author's travels to Persia and Arabia, by Khwajah abd-ul-Karim bin Khwajah Aaqibat Mahmood bin Khwajah Bulaq bin Khwajah Muhammad Reza.

According to the Preface, the Work is divided into five chapters and a Khatimah (Conclusion) each sub divided into several sections. The manuscript is wormed throughout and the margins are badly damaged. Written in an ordinary Nastaliq within coloured ruled borders. Not dated, apparently of 19th century.

A few other manuscripts in Sanskirit and Bengali languages are also considered very rare in terms of quality and content:

- Suddhitattavam
- Vaisnavarandana
- Mitaksara
- Giti kalpah
- Pravaradhaya
- Kalamadhava
- Mulyasangrah
- Nyayakaustubha

Debates: Debates of the House of Lords on the evidence delivered in the trial of Warren Hastings, published in 1797 in London.

Pantographia: Contains accurate copies of all known alphabets in the World by Edmund Fry appeared in 1799 in London on Vellum.

The Ramayunu: A poem in five volumes by Kirtee Bass printed at the Mission Press in 1802 at Serampore. It is the first version of the most popular Bengali translation of the Ramayana.

- Pliny's Naturalis Historia (Parma, 1481)
- Biblia Damulica (Tranquebar, 1723)
- Hicky's Bengal Gazette or Calcutta General Advertiser (1780-1781): the first newspaper of India.

Automation

The website of the Library is designed and hosted by CYBER ANIMA TRIX Private Limited, Kolkata, India. Recently, the National Library developed a more beautiful and informative website which contains many more information about the Library activities as compare to its earlier website.

Under the modernization of Library and informatics programmes for the 7th five year plan, 1985-90, the National Library, Kolkata had decided to automate its technical activities. Accordingly, in consultation with 'the computer experts from the Regional Computer Centre, Jadavpur and National Informatics Centre, Jadavpur, the Library authorities had decided to purchase Hewlett Packard (HP) 3000/37 series computer systems to meet the need of automated library operations.

Computer Division is the youngest division among all the sections of the Library. It was established in 1988 to augment the modernisation activities in the Library. It started with a Mini Computer- HP 3000. MINISIS, RDBMS software was installed for bibliographic control activities. In 2001 the Institution switched over to Client-Server Environment with SUN E450 as the server. At present a Campus Wide Network is being developed with 98 HP Pentium III PCs as nodes. In 2004-05, the fourth phase of National Library Campus Wide Networking (NLLAN) at Bhasha Bhawan has completed. The website of the Library contains bibliographic information of a portion of its holdings with limited fields for ready access by users with following delimitations:

- The records were originally created in MARC 21 format, but due to the pressing needs of users, arrangements have been made to display the records with limited fields.
- Resource sharing at this stage is not possible from this trial data base. However, within the next few months, the users will be able to view the full records in MARC 21 format.
- Bibliographic information of old scanned books has also been put up in a separate database.
- Arrangements have been made for users to view five scanned books every month from now on. Due to some unavoidable reasons, these will be available in parts instead of the whole document as one file.
- Bibliographic information of a part of its holding
- Bibliographic information of scanned books
- Online books of the month
- Online registration
- Online reservation of books
- Feedback through email
- Payment gateways.

Besides, the bibliographic details of manuscripts treasures of our national library can also be viewed at National Mission for Manuscript's (NAMAMI) website.

Digitization: The scanning and archiving of rare and brittle books and other documents on Compact Disc are under taken. English books and documents published before 1900 and Indian publications of pre 1920 are considered for digitisation in its initial phase. So far, 6,600 selected books in Indian and English languages have already been scanned and stored on 548 CDs — a total of over 25,00,000 pages.[47]

The Library has a separate division for Physical, Chemical, Reprographic, and Digital Conservation. Some of the notable titles and earliest books which are already scanned and available on CDs are as follows:

- Documents of East India Company, e.g. Report of the proceedings of the East India Company in regard to the production of cotton wool written in 1788.
- Bengal selection of records written in 1826
- Prabasi - a journal in Bengali
- Land settlement reports
- The famed romance rendered into English by Charles Cottrell written in 1667
- Les voyages de Jean Struys en Muscovite written in 1720
- Calcutta Monthly Magazine written in 1797
- Orunudoi Samvad Patra (a monthly magazine in Assamese) of 1846, 1853, and 1856 – 1858
- Pothi Bhai Valam written 1891 in Punjabi.

In continuing efforts in this direction, the National Library undertook a Pilot project entitled "Down to Memory Lane" to digitize its rare and brittle books in late 90's. In a way, it is an extension of the earlier project, the content being the only difference. The National Library has in its possession a small holding of manuscripts representing some basic and important branches of knowledge.

Other activities

One of the basic functions of the National Library is to conserve the printed heritage to the future generations. For this purpose, the Library has separate divisions for various conservation works like physical conservation, chemical conservation, and reprographic conservation.[48]

The Library also provides an additional service for users. In this connection, it provides counseling and guidance in conservation of library materials and in modernization activities of the libraries to the different institutions on request. Regular courses are conducted in the National Library premises and in various part of India, to impart information in the field.[49]

To cater the needs of children and school goers, the National Library of India has a separate Children Library which houses more than 20,000 printed books during the year 1984-85. With the long passage of time, it must have augmented more and more volumes to this.

To work effectively towards the automated activities and programmes of the National Library, several training sessions, workshops, seminars, conferences etc. were held at the Computer Centre and elsewhere. The technical staff had received elementary training regarding computer applications from the Regional Computer Centre, Jadavpur. Apart from these, several training programmes, meetings and seminars were arranged where the staffs were invited to take active part in the automation programmes of the Library.

The Library possesses approximately 24, 02,579 books and 3, 227 rare and important manuscripts in its collection. The language wise break up of the printed books and manuscripts are as follows:

S. No.	*Language*	*Number of Printed Books*	*Number of Manuscripts*
1.	Assamese	12,000	-
2.	Bengali	85,000	162
3.	Gujarati	37,000	-
4.	Hindi	80,000	05
5.	Kannada	32,000	-
6.	Kashmiri	500	-
7.	Malayalam	34,500	-
8.	Marathi	37,000	-
9.	Oriya	19,500	-
10.	Punjabi		-
11.	Sanskrit, Pali and Prakrit	20,000	790
12.	Sindhi	2,100	-
13.	Tamil	57,000	370
14.	Telugu		-
15.	Urdu	20,000	21
16.	Arabic		681
17.	Persian		955
18.	English		255
	Total Collection	**24, 02,579**	**3,227**

Rampur Raza Library, Rampur

17. Rampur Raza Library, Rampur

Profile of the Library

The Rampur Raza Library is a treasure house of Indo-Islamic learning and Art, founded by Nawab Fazlullah Khan in 1774 A.D. His descendants continued to enrich the collection after the attainment of Independence and merger of the state in the Union of India; the Library was brought under the management of trust till the Government of India took over the Library on first July 1975 under an act of Parliament and declared it as an institution of National Importance. Its affairs are managed by the Rampur Raza Library Board, whose chairman is the H.E. Governor of Utter Pradesh. It is one of the richest libraries in India as far as the oriental language manuscripts and books are concerned. It possesses more or less 80,000 printed books and 15, 000 manuscripts of which most of in Arabic, Urdu and Persian. Rampur Raza Library has a unique collection of manuscripts in Arabic, Persian, Sanskrit, Hindi, Tamil, Pushto, Urdu, Turkish and other languages. The Library, apart from providing the rare manuscripts and literature to the researchers and academicians, organizes lecture and workshops on various themes. Now, the Library has well established and organized Conservation Laboratory that is wedded to the preservation of manuscripts, paintings and art objects. It also has a rich collection of miniature paintings belonging to the Mongol, Mughal, Iranian, Rajput, Kangra, Awadh and Company schools and has acquired the valuable Loharu Collection. The Library has also a collection of about 5,000 miniature paintings and Bhoj Patras and an album of 3,000 specimens of mater calligraphers of Central Asia, Iran and India.

Publications

The Library has publishes so far over 66 titles on various subjects edited by eminent personalities. It includes descriptive catalogues, descriptive abstracts on rare manuscripts and number of other subjects. Most of the publications of the Library concerned with its rare and world famous manuscripts. Rampur Raza Library has a separate unit which publishes the abstracts of rare manuscripts on Indian culture, Islamic literature, Medieval Indian History, and Oriental Studies etc. in different oriental languages including Hindi, Arabic, Persian, Sanskrit etc. The Library has published 12 manuscripts dealing with history and is preparing a critical edition of *Tarikh-e-Baburi*, a manuscript of immense historical value. The book is a contemporary Persian translation by the courtier Zain-e-Khanafi. *Tarikh-e-*

Mohammadi, another important text, is being transcribed from the original for publication.

Renowned Manuscripts

The Library preserves world famous and rare manuscripts in its collection. It is basically famous for its nice collection of manuscripts in oriental languages e.g. Arabic, Persian, Urdu, Hindi, Sanskrit etc. The Library has also retains world famous and earliest copy of the Holy Quran dates back of 7th century and written on parchment in Kufic Script attributed to Fourth Caliph of Islam, Hadhrat Ali.[50]

The Conservation Laboratory has been attending to the damaged manuscripts, old books, Mughal miniature paintings, historical documents, old photographs and other art objects. The Laboratory treated 214 objects including 4972 pages of manuscripts till 2005.

During the period 2009-10, 1, 184 Persian manuscripts has been completed by the preventive conservation, 3070 pages from 08 rare printed books 07 miniature paintings, 404 pages from 1 manuscript have been conserved scientifically. The reviews conducted by the Ministry during the last two years led to the assessment that the Library has been successful in undertaking its work assigned to it.

The Library houses some of the rarest manuscripts in its collection which are worthy to mention here:

Holy Quran (7th Century) : Some of the Arabic collections may be considered as the oldest pieces of handiwork in the field of Arabic Calligraphy. Among them is the seventh century A.D. Quran written on parchment in early Kufic script attributed to Hazrat Ali, the fourth caliph of Islam. (D. A.D. 661).

Kaleela Wa Dimna: Believed to be written in the 16th century A.D., this copy of the manuscript was finally illustrated by Abul Maali Nasrullah bin Muhammad bin Abdul Hamid al-Ghaznavi. The paintings depict landscapes, fauna, flora, court scenes, among others and are accompanied by in Persian language and Nastaliq script.

Probodh Chandrika: Among the notable Sanskrit manuscripts, mention may be made of Probodh Chandrika, a work on grammar. It was written by Baijnath Dev Chauhan Vanshi and scribed by Girdhari Lal Mishra. There is an important but incomplete commentary on Jyotish Ratanmala written by Shri Shripati Bhatta. An interesting work entitled Natrajan Dipmishada on Karma Kanda or Stuart also contains certain mantras for brightening the eyesight. The Mahinma Statures is a very famous work with commentary compiled by Pushpa Dutta with commentator Madhusudan Saraswati.

Ajaibul Makhluqat wa Gharibul Maujudat: *Written in 1571 A.D. in Arabic using the Naskh script, this is a rare and illustrated copy of a work that describes the wonders of the World.*

Ramayana: This Persian translation of the classic epic was carried out by Sumir Chand in 1715 A.D. It consists of 675 folios and 258 illustrations.

Apart from the above mentioned texts, the Library kept following many more masterpieces of manuscripts in its possession:

- *Tarikh-e-Mohammadi*
- Risala-e-Tanseni
- *Tarikh-e-Baburi*
- Suwar–al-Kawakib
- Jahangir Naama
- Akbar Naama
- Padshah Naama
- Jami-al –Tawarikh
- Jam-e-Jamm by Ahmad Khan Bahadur B.S. Muhammad Muttaqi Dehlawi
- Farhang-e-Jahangiri by S. Jamal-ud-Din Husain Shirazi
- Jawahir-ut-Tahqeeq by Mulla Ghayasuddin Izzat bin Jalaluddin Rampuri
- Hidayat-ul-Meezan by Safi-ud-Din bin Nasir-ud-Din Jaunpuri

- Kifayat-us-Sarf by Abdul Qadir bin Muhammad Adil bin Shaikh Usmani
- Khazanah Amirah by Mir Ghulam Ali Azad Bilgrami
- Mizan-al-Huruf by Muhammad Husain bin Husain
- Anis-ush-Shuara by Abdul Karim known as Karimi
- Kitab-e-Lughat by S. Najaf Ali khan bin .S.M. Azim-ud-Din
- Gulistan-i-Hind by Raja Durga Prasad Sandelvi
- Tarikh-e-Firoz Shahi by Ziauddin Burni
- Rahat-ul-Qulub by Shaikh Nizamuddin-Din M. bin Ahmad Badayuni Dehlawi
- Diwan-i-Mubram Shah by Mubram Siyah Qazwini
- Diwan-i-Hafiz by Khwaja Shams-ud-Din Muhammad Shirazi
- Tuti Namah by Zia-ud-Din Naqshabi Albadwani.

A folio from mss. Kaleela wa Dimna, RRL, Rampur(courtesy : NMAMI)

Two folios from mss. Persian Ramayana, RRL, Rampur (courtesy:NAMAMI)

Automation

The Library has implemented its own LAN (Local Area Network) to interlink the computers available in different sections of the Library to unite the total potential of the computers and therefore to increase the working efficiency of the Library. This activity also has minimized the use of external storage media in the Library and therefore, there is minimum risk of data-loss in case of breakdown of any computer. During period 2004-05, around 48, 620 Hindi, Urdu, Arabic, English and Persian books have been computerized using the software "CollecSys" which is the best known oriental cataloging software.[51]

During the period under report the Library has done cataloguing of 40,000 Urdu, Arabic, and Persian books, and 10,000 English books and 2,000 Hindi with the help of above mentioned software. The Library has also installed an OPAC system to enable scholars and users to access the digitized database of the books in the Library. The OPAC of the Library can also be searched through its website.[52]

The miniatures paintings, masterpieces, colored and calligraphy based title pages of world renowned manuscripts and rarest among the rare printed books of medieval India can be seen on its website which is developed by NIC.

The bibliographic details about important manuscripts of this Library can be accessed using manuscripts database created by National Mission for Manuscripts (NAMAMI) on its website.

Digitization

The Library has made a remarkable progress in its objectives towards automating the Library and digitizing its collection of rare books and manuscripts. Also, it is during the year 2004-05, the Library has seen the unbound progression towards a High Tech Library. During the above mentioned period, digitization and preparing of CD's of rare paintings, specimens of Islamic Calligraphy, precious illustrated manuscripts, art objects and coins has been completed. About 42, 000 images from 40 albums of paintings, 85 albums of Islamic Calligraphy and 195 illustrated and non-illustrated manuscripts so far, scanned with detailed information.[53]

The MRC at Rampur Raza Library has been functioning since August 2003. The MRC has so far documented 43, 300 manuscripts of Urdu, Arabic and Persian languages. It has covered 40 institutions and 100 private collections covering 60 districts during Survey and has held 7 awareness campaigns.

The MCC has so far taken preventive care of 13,081 manuscripts and given curative conservation treatment to 3,933 manuscripts.[54]

Other Activities

From time to time, the Library has also organized seminars, workshops and Mushayira (recitation of Urdu poems by Poets in any Function). The Library also engaged in display of its paintings and rare manuscripts on special occasions. The Raza Library's most valuable and rare miniature paintings and manuscripts, selected for an exhibition (on Mughal nobleman Bairam Khan), was displayed at the National Archives of India, New Delhi.

During the period 2009-10, 65 research scholars consulted 363 manuscripts, 3,112 printed books were issued by 1,097 readers.

The language wise break up of printed books and manuscripts in the Library are as follows:

S. No.	*Language*	*Number of Printed Documents*	*Number of Manuscripts*
1.	Arabic	5802	5502
2.	Persian	5261	4271
3.	Urdu	26382	1781
4.	Hindi	1410	665
5.	Turkish and Pushto	144	45
6.	Loharu collection	2942	444
7.	Palm leaves	-	205
8.	English	7747	-
9.	Marathi	01	-
10.	Punjabi	14	-
11.	French	17	-
12.	German	32	-
13.	Russian	10	-
14.	Sanskrit	174	-
15.	Others	204	-
	Total Collection	**80,000**	**15,000**

Shri D. K. Jain Oriental Research Institute, Arrah

18. Shri D. K. Jain Oriental Research Institute, Arrah

Profile of the Library

The "Jain Sidhanta Bhawan" better known as the "Central Jain Oriental Library, Arrah" was found in 1903 by Sri Dev Kumar Jain, a great scholar and philanthropist. The Library has a valuable collection of manuscripts from all over the world. There are 3,179 palm leaf manuscripts, 3,500 paper manuscripts which are at least 500 years old. Besides the manuscripts, the library has 9,000 published books on religion, philosophy, history, and literature in nearly all the Indian and some foreign languages. There is also a collection of old paintings, pieces of art and old coins. Most prominent among the manuscript collection are the illustrated *Jain Ramayana* and the *Bhaktamira*. There are nearly 200 paintings in *Jain Ramayana* alone in excellent Mughul and Rajput styles. Among the paintings on mythological subjects, treatment of the 16 dreams of Chandragupta, the 16 Tirthankars and Pawapuri temple stand out.

Publications

A research biannual journal "The Jain Antiquary" is being published since 1953.

Renowned Manuscripts

The Institute preserves following very important and rare manuscripts in its library:

Tatwarth Sutra: It is a palm leaf manuscript written by Shri Uma Swamy. Contains only one folio and it is one of the few complete manuscripts of the Institute. Written in Kannada and subject of the manuscript is Darshana.

Swayamdut Srota: Written by Shri Samanta Bhadracharya on paper and contains only one folio. The script of the manuscript is Kannada and thought content carries religious discourses.

Samudra Natak: It is a palm leaf manuscript on Poetry as well as Drama. Written by Shri Hast Mallji. Written in Kannada script and contains only one folio.

Phadikumar Charitra: It is also a palm leaf manuscript and written by Shri Kalyan Kirti. The language of the manuscript is Kannada and contents encompass poetical verses. The taxt contains only one folio.

Nyaya Sarpad Punjika: Though, it is an incomplete manuscript but written on palm leaf. Text contains poetical verses in Kannada language. Written by Vasu Dev Jee and contains one folio.

Prakrima Sangrah: It is a Kannada language manuscript written by Shri Sankatayan on palm leaf. It is incomplete text and contains only one folio. The subject of the manuscript is Grammer.

Kriyakandchulika: It is a Kannada manuscript written by Shri Paddha Nandi on the subject of Jainism. Though, it is incomplete but written on palm leaf and contains only one folio.

Automation

The Institute has its own website which contains some very useful information about it. But, it is not clear whether the Institute's library has been modernized or not till date. The Online Public Access Catalogue (OPAC) or any information about its valulable printed books and rare manuscripts are not available in its website. Though, bibliographic information of its manuscripts has been included in NAMAMI manuscripts database.

Digitization

The MRC at the Sri D. K. Jain Oriental Research Institute has been functioning since May 2005. Since then the MRC is engaged in documenting manuscripts and producing electronic data with the help of 8 scholars and 6 official staff in 15 districts. The MRC has so far documented 1, 15,464 manuscripts, in electronic format including Post Survey documentation. Manuscripts found in these districts are mostly written in *Devanagari, Urdu, Maithili,* and *Bengali* covering wide range of subjects like *Veda, Vedanta, Darshana, Karmakanda* and many other such subjects. The MCC of the Mission has already provided both curative and preventive conservation treatment to 2,2,38,533 folios till date. Two awareness programmes organized by the MRC has rendered help to the people in preserving and sharing their knowledge about the manuscripts. It has also documented **56,410** Jain manuscripts under the Register of Jain Manuscripts scheme which data is integrated with the National Electronic Database. The Institute has also coordinated the National Survey for Manuscripts in 22 districts of Bihar till date and is now looking after the Post Survey programme in those districts.[55]

Other activities

The research scholars wcrking here have been awarded Ph. D and DLitt. Degrees. Presently, a few research scholars are working on Jain Sanskrit Anthology, 'Doha' Literature in Apabhramsha, the Jain poetry in Sanskrit and poet Rayadhu of the Apabhramsba literature.

Salar Jung Museum and Library, Hyderabad

19. Salar Jung Museum and Library, Hyderabad

Profile of the Library

The Salar Jung Museum and Library, Hyderabad, is a repository of artefacts, printed documents and rare manuscripts. It houses over 57, 882 books and rare manuscripts from across the world. The major portion of this collection was acquired by Nawab Mir Yousuf Ali khan, the eponymous Salar Jung III, but a few were also inherited by him from his father Salar Jung II, Nawab Mir Laiq Ali khan, and his grandfather Salar Jung I, Nawab Mir Turab Ali khan. This vast personal collection was opened to the public by the then Prime Minister of India, Pundit Jawaharlal

Nehru on 16 December 1951. In 1961, the Museum has been declared as an Institution of National Importance through an Act of Parliament and its administration entrusted to an autonomous Board of Trustees with the governor of Andhra Pradesh as ex-officio chairman.[56]

The Museum was declared as an Institution of national importance in 1961. It is a fully funded autonomous body under the Ministry of Culture. It is engaged in conservation, preservation, acquisition of art objects of historical importance and educational activities such as organizing exhibitions, popular lectures, gallery talks, seminars etc. The main functions of the Museum are collection, preservation, organizing exhibitions, conducting research, educational and publication activities. To keep the reserve collection some of the Stores have been reorganized on modern and scientific lines. The Museum is engaged in exhibiting its art collection to the visiting public apart from organizing variety of educational and cultural programmes based on the contents of the Museum.

Publications

To meet the needs of scholars and research students and also interested visitors, the Museum has been publishing catalogues on certain important collections of its Library. So far, it has come out with catalogues on Persian, Arabic and Urdu manuscripts, special monographs, apart from the 'SJM Bi-Annual Research Journal' to facilitate the researchers.Museum publications, including popular leaflets and picture postcards of the collection are sold at the publication sales counter.

Apart from the above mentioned publications, a number of individuals publishes descriptive catalogue and treatises on manuscripts treasure of this Library.

1. Kutubkhanah Nawab Salar Jang Marhoom ki Urdu Qalami Kitabon ki Wazahati Fihrist. Compiled by Nasiruddin Hashimi, Hyderabad, Ibrahimiya Press, 1957.

2. A catalogue of Arabic manuscripts in the Salar Jung Museum and Library, vols. 1-8. Compiled by Muhammad Nizamuddin and Muhammad Ashraf, Hyderabad, SJML, 1957-2000.
3. A Concise descriptive catalogue of Persian manuscripts in the Salar Jung Museum and Library, vols. 1-12. Compiled by Muhammad Ashraf. Hyderabad, SJML, 1965-2007.

Renowned Manuscripts

The manuscripts collection forms an important section of the Library which in turn is a part of the Museum. It has been stated that "it is the second largest centre of manuscripts in Andhra Pradesh and compare favorably with other centers spread all over the world as regards the Arabic, Persian and Urdu manuscripts are concerned". This treasure of manuscripts consists of more than 8,500 in Arabic, Persian and Urdu languages. In addition to these three major languages, the collection also contains Hindi, Turkish, and Pushto Manuscripts. This collection also includes nearly 1,200 loose panels of calligraphy.[57]

The noteworthy possessions of manuscripts in the organisation are:

Padmawat: A Persian version of Malik Muhammad Jaisi's Hindi poem called Padmawat, compiled by Sayyid Muhammad bin Yusuf al Husaini, pen name, Ishrati. It is the story of Rat (or Ratansen) and Padmawati. This work was compiled during the reign of Alamgir for the author's son, Sayyid Ahmad in the year 1110 A.H.

Waqiyat-e-Kashmir: It deals with the detailed history of Kashmir from the earliest time down to 1160 A.H./1747 A.D., by Muhammad Azam bin Khair-uz-Zaman Khan. The work was started in 1148 A.H., the title bring the chronogram and dedicated to the Emperor Muhammad Shah. It was, however, compiled after twelve years as given in the Masnavi at the end, in which the chronogram is found in couplet. Also contains refrences of mystics and poets of Kashmir.

Siyar-ul-Muluk: A treatise on Political Science compiled by Khwaja Nizam-ul-Mulk written in the year 1028 A.H./ 1619 A.D. The work is dedicated to Sultan Said Muhammad bin Malik Shah Saljuqi, transcribed in good Nastaliq in Persian.

Diwan-e-Quli Qutb Shah: It is poetic work in the Urdu written by the founder of Hyderabad, Muhammad Quli Qutb Shah. It is one of the prized possessions of the Library. A few copies are available in the library of SJML.

Tarjuma-e-Minhaj-al-Bayan: Persian paraphrases of Ibn Jazla's Arabic treatise on Medicine by Muhammad bin Muhammad Ar-Radd-at-Tabib. Ibn Iazla who was a Christian converted to Islam, adopted Yahya bin Isa as his name. It is a glossary of simple Medicines, Drinks and Diets compiled in 679 A.H./1280 A.D. The work also happens to be one of the oldest of Persian manuscripts in the SJML.

Ikhtiyarat-e-Qutb Shahi: The SJML preserves two beautiful copies of this Work is a critical study of the famous Ikhtiyatat-e-Baddi, compiled by Mir Muhammad Mumin-al-Astrabadi and other Hakims (expert in Unanui Medicine) on the orders of Sultan Muhammad Quli Qutb Shah, the founder of the erstwhile Hyderabad. Transcribed in fine Nastaliq by Muhammad Mumin known as 'Arab-ash-Shirazi with excellent 'Unwans (headings) and Marginal Decorations'in the year 1040 A.H./1630 A.D.

Siraj-al-Lisan: A versified vocabulary of Persian works with their equivalents in Telugu, compiled in 1142 A.H. /1730 A.D. by Shah Safiullah, pen-name 'Safi'. The manuscript is written in Shikasta Nastaliq, but, undeniably a rare and invaluable work on the Subject.

Holy Quran: The most precious copies of the Quran Collection in the Museum were transcribed by Yakut-al-Mustasami in April, 1283 A.D. It contains the autographs of Emperors Jahangir, Shah Jahan and Aurangzeb at the beginning.

Tahafat-al-Falasifah by Imam Ghazzali: The oldest manuscripts of SJML collection is perhaps the Mss. entitled 'Tahafat-al-Falasifah' written by none other than convincing proof of Islam(popularly known in the West by the Orientalists), Imam Ghazzali. It was written in the year 1113 A.D. The said manuscript contains discussions on Islamic and Greek philosophy at length.

To keep the reserve collection, some of the Stores have been reorganized on modern and scientific lines. The work of up gradation of Library and conservation of manuscripts/ documents/books was continued by the Museum during the years 2007-08 and 2008-09. Digital documentation of 25,000 objects was undertaken by the Museum during the period.[58]

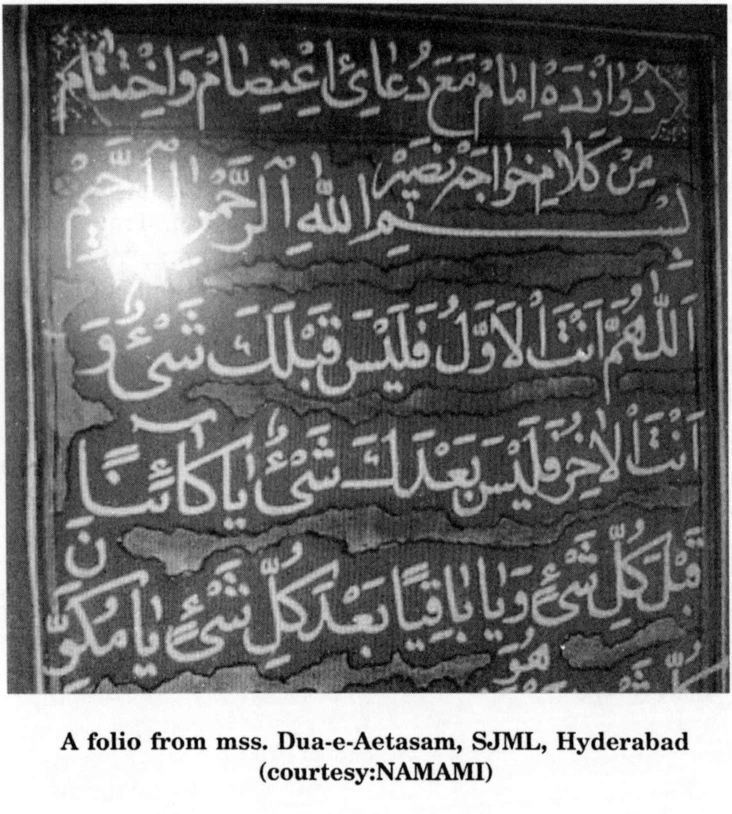

A folio from mss. Dua-e-Aetasam, SJML, Hyderabad (courtesy:NAMAMI)

Two folios from a mss. , SJML, Hyderabad (courtesy:NAMAMI)

Automation

The work of up gradation of Library and conservation of manuscripts/documents/books was continued by the Museum during the years 2007-08 and 2008-09. Digital documentation of 25, 000 objects was undertaken by the Museum during the period. CCTV in all galleries and Fire Alarm System were installed during the period under review.

Apart from its own initiatives in the direction of automation, the National Mission for Manuscripts is also assisting the Library. One can see the bibliographic details of manuscripts of this Library on Mission's Manuscripts Database using its website.

Digitization

It will be possible soon to access the rich collection of the Library of India's famous Salar Jung Museum and Library, from the comfort of one's drawing room. This has become possible with the project of converting all the Museum's books into digital format. For this purpose, six scanners and twenty computers have been installed to store the pages in digital format.

The Museum possesses over 57,882 printed books and invaluable 9, 000 manuscripts. This is a part of the Digital Library of India (DLI) project to digitize one million books by 2007. The project is in collaboration with Carnegie Mellon University, Pittsburgh. One million books in Indian language would be put on the web so that these may be accessed by anyone, anywhere,

It would take at least one and a half-years to digitize all the Museum books. About 60 to 100 books would be scanned daily. Not just books, even art objects in the Museum would be digitized. "Anyone will be able to take a virtual tour of the Museum," Dr. Raj Reddy said.

The Museum authorities are by and large in favour of allowing cameras into the Museum as it would fulfil a long demand besides adding to the revenue of the Museum. The digitization of museum holdings may be very fruitful in the light of its visitors every day. As such, about 5, 000 persons on an average visit the Museum daily and during holidays this figure crosses 10, 000. Visitors from all over the world come here and feel deprived when they are not allowed to carry cameras inside. However, it is feared that too much use of camera flash light could prove hazardous to paintings and miniatures. But, there would be no problem with other objects. From security point of view too, there would be no problems.[59]

Keeping pace with the changing technology, the Museum undertook the process of digitalization of rare books and manuscripts a few years back and is making a steady progress in this endeavor.

The Library has many rare and precious books in English, Urdu, Arabic, Persian and Turkish which need to be preserved in digital form for future generations. Recently, the SJML has entered into a MoU with International Institute of Information Technology (IIIT), Hyderabad for digitization of books and manuscripts. It will provide the equipment namely Scanners, Computers etc. IIIT is undertaking this work under the Digital Library project initiated by Carnegie Mellon University, Pittsburgh, USA. The infrastructure has been provided by the Museum and the equipment and manpower is being provided by the IIIT. The project is likely to be completed in 3 years of time. The lists of all rare and precious books have been prepared and the scanning is in progress. So far 22, 000 books have been scanned and around 8,000 books have been put on its website.[60]

The importance being attached with digital concepts, the remarks given by following concerned authorities, it is hoped that, this Library will be converted into a Virtual Digital Library soon. "These books are very old and valuable books. The idea of digitalization is that most of the scholars visit Salar Jung Library, whenever the scholar comes, the book he wants to access through the digital library comes on the computer," said, Dr. Nagender Reddy, Joint Director Salar Jung Museum.

The process of digitalization is intricate as one has to be very careful while scanning these rare books and manuscripts because they are very old and there is a danger of them being damaged. A. Swathi, who currently is Head (In charge) of the Digital Library, spoke about the digitalization procedure. "First we get books which are old and we scan them. After that we process them and spell check. When we do the scanning we have to be careful because these pages are very old. The digitalisation is an effort to save these rare manuscripts for the posterity.

The Museum began its association with National Mission for Manuscripts as an MCC in October 2003 for the conservation of manuscripts in Andhra Pradesh. It has a well equipped conservation laboratory. It has so far taken preventive care of 11,883 manuscripts and given curative conservation treatment to 2,085 manuscripts.

The Salar Jung Museum and Library has begun its association with the Mission as an MCC in October 2003 for the conservation of manuscripts in the state of Andhra Pradesh. The centre of the Mission has provided preventive and curative conservation treatment to 19 institutes covering both, palm leaf and paper manuscripts. The Centre has also successfully undertaken curative conservation of 1, 14,264 folios along with preventive conservation of 49268 folios in various collections.[61]

Other Activities

Seminars and workshops are organized in the Museum and Library usually on the occasions of birthday celebrations of Salar Jung III, Museum Week, and Children's Week etc. as part of its educational activities. The Museum organizes temporary exhibitions periodically on various themes and efforts are being made to make them more aesthetic, educative and informative. As a part of regular events, the museum conducted 21 temporary exhibitions, 3 seminars, 2 workshops and 13 lectures during the year 2007-08 whereas in 2008-09, the Museum conducted 23 temporary exhibitions, 2 seminars, 1 workshop and 16 lectures. During the year 2007-08, two galleries were re-organized. In 2008-09, 2 new galleries were re-organized and the re-organization work for 2 galleries is in progress. CCTV in all galleries and Fire

Alarm System were installed during the period under review.[62]

As per report of working group on Art and Culture for XI Five-Year Plan and Proposals for XI Five-Year Plan (2007-12) and Annual Plan (2007-08) Ministry of Culture, Government of India, New Delhi, January, 2007, the following galleries have been re organized on modern and scientific methods to match with international standards by the Salar Jung Museum and Library:

- European clock gallery
- Chinese gallery
- Japanese gallery
- French gallery
- European Porcelain
- Glass gallery

It is also maintaining a 'Mobile Exhibition Van' arranging exhibits on different themes on the Museum's Collections and the Cultural heritage of India to present the Museum at the doorstep of schools, villages and other public places as part of Museum Education.[63]

The language wise break up of the printed books and manuscripts in major oriental languages are as follows:

S.No.	*Language*	*Number of Printed Books*	*Number of Manuscripts*
1.	Arabic	2,500	2,500
2.	Persian	3,500	4,700
3.	Urdu	13,000	1, 200
4.	English	40,000	-
5.	Turkish	160	-
	Total collection	**57,882**	**9,000**

20. Scindia Oriental Research Institute (SORI)at Vikram Kirti Mandir, Ujjain

Scindia Oriental Research Institute (SORI), Ujjain

Profile of the Library

Scindia Oriental Research Institute, Ujjain, Madhya Pradesh is situated within the Vikram Kirti Mandir. It is a pioneer manuscript library of India and ranked 11th in India as per the Indian National Trust for Art and Cultural Heritage (INTACH) Survey.

Maharaja Jiwaji Rao Scindia set up a committee in 1938 under the Chairmanship of Sir Manu Bhai Desai with Dr. Radhankrishnan, Dr. Amaranth Jha and Professor Paranjbe as its members to establish permanent memory of Maharaja Vikram celebrating Vikram era festival. The committee recommended establishment of Vikram University, Vikram Kirti Mandir including Archeological Museum, Scindia Oriental Research Institute and a Conference hall. During independence movement, it was delayed. In 1941, Vikram Bi-Centenary festival was organized in Ujjain when the earlier oriental book collection was renamed as Scindia Oriental Institute and was included in normal budget of education department of Gwalior State for financial help. Then President of India Dr. Rajendra

Prasad laid foundations of Vikram Kirti Mandir on 8th May, 1951. But due to delay in its progress, the Scindia Oriental Research Institute was transferred in a rental house- Nawab Sahib Bangla near Madhav Club. After state reorganization in 1956 and establishment of newly carved Madhya Pradesh, the SORI were transferred to the control of Deputy Director of School Education in M.P. Government. Finally Vikram University was established in 1957 and on 6th November, 1960 a Memorandum of Understanding (MoU) was signed between M.P Govt. and Vikram University. On 26th June, 1961 the Institute was transferred to the Vikram University. In 1966, it was shifted to newly constructed Jiwaji Rao Library building. Finally, in August, 1968, after construction of some parts of Vikram Kirti Mandir, the Institute was shifted to its own place.

Publications

The Institute has published the following titles under the 'Scindia Oriental Series':

1. Tattvasara (Marathi), 1936, 414p.
2. Alankara Manjusha, 1940, 384p.
3. Ancient Jaina Hymns, 1951, 178p.
4. Sastrattva Vinirnaya, 1952, 136p.
5. Chikitsa Manjari, 1959, 206p.
6. Journal of Scindia Oriental Institute, Vol. I, 1955
7. Journal of Scindia Oriental Institute, Vol. II, 1956
8. A descriptive catalogue of manuscripts in the Scindia Oriental Institute, Vol. II, (literature), Part-I, 1983, 282p.
9. A descriptive catalogue of manuscripts in the Scindia Oriental Institute, Vol. II, (literature), Part-II, 1985, 414p.
10. Vikram Volume (English), 768p.
11. Vikram Smriti Grantha (Hindi), 927p.
12. Vikram Smriti Grantha (Marathi), 568p.

Renowned Manuscripts

The Institute houses around 18,695 manuscripts mostly in the languages of Sanskrit, Prakrit, Arabic, Persian and other Indian languages and covers a wide range of subjects from Vedic Literature and Philosophy to Dance and Music. Most of the manuscripts are available in Sanskrit language but the other manuscripts are written in many languages like Marathi, Hindi, Gujrati, Arabic, Persian, Bengali, Maithili and Telugu etc. Many kinds of writing materials can be seen here like papers, palm leaves, birch barks, metal plates etc.

There is a separate Reference Library of important oriental publications and a rich collection of old paintings in the Rajput and Mughal style. The Institute also houses Palm leaf and bark leaf manuscripts and an illustrated manuscript of Srimad Bhagavata. Only, a small portion of the present collection of manuscripts was made available from Ujjain, remaining collection was brought from different places mainly from Lashkar, Gwalior, Mandsaur, Poona, Jalgaon, Sagar, Ratnagiri, Banaras, Jalone, Indore and Srinagar (Kashmir).

The following few manuscripts are noteworthy to mention here:

- Sawatam Sukh by Aik Naath
- Kayasath Dharamdeep by Baba Bhatt
- Karma Wapika by Govinda
- Utsargamayukh by Neel Kantha Bhatt
- Sawatimanripun by Shankaracharya
- Swarup Prakash by Sada Nanda.

Automation

There is urtgent need to do sturdy efforts in the direction of Computerization/Automation which help the users to get the acess of this great Library.

Digitization

The Manuscript Resource Centre at Scindia Oriental Research Institute, Vikram University, Ujjain, started functioning in September 2003. The MRC has conducted extensive survey and documentation in the state of Madhya Pradesh and prepared electronic data of **38,840** manuscripts which have been integrated into the Manus Granthavali Software of the Mission. The Institute has so far covered ninety (90) institutions and thirty four (34) private collections covering twenty two (22) districts throughout Madhya Pradesh. The data received from these institutions and private collections was on a variety of manuscripts on paper, palm leaf, and birch bark written in Sanskrit and Hindi languages. The Scindia oriental research institute signed a MoU with the Mission on June 15, 2006. The emphasis of the MCC was only on preventive conversation. It has provided both curative and preventive conservation treatment to 6, 06, 963 palm leaf folios.[64]

Other Activities

Apart from having a very good library, the Institute maintains an attractive museum in its premises. The Museum also exhibits a rich array of images, inscriptions, copper plates and fossils discovered in the Narmada Valley. A huge skull of a primitive elephant is the major attraction. The above mentioned Museum and an Art Gallery are major repositories of heritage items and artifacts.

21. Tawang Monastery, Tawang

Tawang Monastery, Tawang

Profile of the Library

The Tawang Monastery was founded near the small town of the same name in the north western part of Arunachal Pradesh, India, by Merak Lama Lodre Gyatso during 1680-1681. The Monastery belongs to the Gelugpa School and has a religious association with Drepung Monastery in Lhasa, which continued during the period of British rule. It is very close to the Tibetan border, located in the valley of the Tawang-chu which flows down from Tibet.[65]

It is located at an elevation of 10,000 feet in Tawang Town in the north-eastern state of Arunachal Pradesh. It is the largest centre for Buddhist cultural studies and also the largest Buddhist monastery in India and second largest in Asia. The Monastery is locally known as 'Tawang Gaden Namgyal Lhatse' or Celestial Paradise of the Divine site chosen by the horse. Tawang Monastery was honoured as 'The Spiritual Wonder of India' by NDTV Seven Wonders of India campaign on March 31, 2009.

It houses the three-storied Parkhang Library, a collection of 400-year-old Kangyur scriptures in addition to many other invaluable manuscripts. Other large collections include the Sutras, Tangym, Sungbhum, old books and other manuscripts, both handwritten and printed, many of them in gold. Dances and Ceremonial Celebrations are held in the courtyard, the most important of which is held on the night of Buddha Poornima. The Library is also housing old scriptures (mainly Kanjur and Tanjur numbering 850 bundles).

Publications

Apart from having a nice library, the Monastery has also houses a small Printing Press.

Renowned Manuscripts

The Tawang Monastery in Arunachal Pradesh houses more than five thousand Buddhist manuscripts in the Parkhang (Library) of the Tawang Monastery. These manuscripts are written in Boti (Tibetan) language and are scattered around few districts as well as under private custody. The Monastery Library contains two printed sets of Tanjur, three sets of Kanjur and five volumes of Changia Sungbum. Each set of Tanjur contains 225 volumes. Among the three sets of Kanjur, two sets are hand written and one set printed. The printed set extends to 101 volumes. One handwritten set has 131 volumes and the other 125volumes. The letters of the letter set are washed with pure gold. Some of them are written with silver. There are three pages of the religious text, called Gyetongpa, embossed throughout in letters of gold is kept in the museum. Many of these valuable manuscripts are brittle and edges are broken. The wood protections on both the sides of these manuscripts eaten by wood borer insects and some of these manuscripts have got bores or holes in between, caused by these wood borers. The origins of these manuscripts are not ascertained since there are no records. The hand written manuscripts are very fragile in nature, some of them are almost in ramshackle conditions. These manuscripts are to be digitized and preserved before decaying further. There are more than one hundred eight Gompas in the Tawang area alone. Each Gompas has several manuscripts preserved in their custody. Apart from these, there are thousands of such manuscript collections in individual position as well. The sacred manuscripts (Pechas) are kept on pigeonholed racks on both the sides of the altar as well as on the northern and southern sides of the hall.

Automation

Though automation work has not been initiated in the Library but the Monastery has maintaning a Website which contains almost all relevant information about it.

Digitization

It is also a designated 'Manuscript Conservation Centre' (MCC) under the National Mission for Manuscripts established in 2003. The Tawang Monastery signed a MoU with the National Mission for Manuscripts on 1st August 2006.

Other Activities

The most fascinating part is the Dukhang or Assembly Hall - a three-storied building housing the temple and the 8.3 m (27 ft) high Golden Buddha. To the left of the altar on the northern wall is a silver casket wrapped in silk containing the Thankas of Goddess Dri Devi (Palden Lhamo), the principal deity of the Monastery. It was given to Merak Lama by the 5th Dalai Lama and has come to be known as the Ja-Droi-Ma, which means it has the warmth of a bird, symbolizing that the Thankas is of a living type.

There is also a Center for Buddhist Cultural Studies where young monks are taught Arithmetic, English and Hindi as well as their traditional monastic education.

The Monastery is three stories high and houses sixty five (65) residential buildings in addition to the Library. It controls seventeen (17) gompas and a few nunneries in the region. It was renovated in 1997 by the 14th Dalai Lama with renovation meaning that the traditionally built structure was torn down and then rebuilt with concrete.

The present Gyalsey Rinpochey, a famous incarnation of the Loseling College of Drepung Monastery, and incarnate head of Tawang, lives and teaches at Tawang.[66]

Notes

1. www.manuscriptlibrary.ap.nic.in
2. Ibid

3. Ibid
4. Chapter VI, Ministry of Culture, Government of India, 2009-10
5. www.asiaticsocietycal.com
6. Gaur, Ramesh C. and Chakraborty, Mrinmoy. Preservation and Access to Indian Manuscripts Heritage Resources of Indian Cultural Resources for Academic Libraries.
7. www.asiaticsocietycal.com
8. Ibid
9. Wikipedia: the free encyclopedia
10. Ibid
11. Ibid
12. Report of the Working Group on Art and Culture for XI five Year Plan (2007-12) and Annual Plan (2007-08), Ministry of Culture, Government of India, January, 2007.
13. www.bori.ac.in
14. Seventh Annual Report (2009-10), National Mission for Manuscripts.
15. Report of the Working Group on Art and Culture for XI five Year Plan (2007-12) and Annual Plan (2007-08), Ministry of Culture, Government of India, January, 2007.
16. Ibid
17. Ibid
18. Seventh Annual Report (2009-10), National Mission for Manuscripts.
19. Report of the Working Group on Art and Culture for XI five Year Plan (2007-12) and Annual Plan (2007-08), Ministry of Culture, Government I, January, 2007.
20. Wikipedia: the free encyclopedia
21. www.connemarapubliclibrarychennai.com
22. Ibid
23. Abidi, Rupa. A Pir and his Priceless Possessions. July 15, 2009 (www.IndianMuslims.in)
24. Annual Report.2004-05, Ministry of Culture, Government of India, p.63-65
25. Ibid

26. Chapter VI, Ministry of Culture, Government of India.
27. Annual Report, 2004-05, Ministry of Culture, Government of India, p. 63-64.
28. Amjad Ali, Oriental Libraries of India and their Collections. p. 71.
29. Sujatha, Gurram. Digital Library Initiative in India: A proposal for Open Distance Learning on April 21-24, 2008 in 29th IATUL Annual Conference, Auckland.
30. Annual Report, 2004-05, Ministry of Culture, p. 64.
31. Varatharajan N. and Chandrasekara, M. Digital library initiatives at Higher Education and Research Institutions in India, Library Philosophy and Practice, 2007.
32. TNN, December 18, 2002.
33. Seventh Annual Report (2009-10) National Mission for Manuscripts.
34. Amjad Ali,Oriental Libraries of India and their Collections. p. 73.
35. LTWA Newsletter, Vol. 1, Fall- 2008.
36. Amjad Ali,Oriental Libraries of India and their Collections. p. 120-121.
37. Seventh Annual Report (2009-10) National Mission for Manuscripts.
38. Raju, A.A.N., Documentary Heritage of Indian Libraries. p. 110-111.
39. Ibid. p. 119.
40. Report of the Working Group on Art and Culture for XI five Year Plan (2007-12) and Annual Plan (2007-08), Ministry of Culture, Government of India, January, 2007.
41. Raju, A.A.N., Documentary Heritage of Indian Libraries. p. 119
42. Ibid. p. 122.
43. Seventh Annual Report (2009-10) National Mission for Manuscripts.
44. Raju, A.A.N., Documentary Heritage of Indian Libraries. p. 119.
45. Report of the Working Group on Art and Culture for XI five Year Plan (2007-12) and Annual Plan (2007-08), Ministry of Culture, Government of India, January, 2007.

46. www.nlindia.org
47. Varatharajan N. and Chandrasekara, M. Digital library initiatives at Higher Education and Research Institutions in India, Library Philosophy and Practice, 2007.
48. www.nlindia.org
49. Ibid.
50. Amjad Ali, Oriental Libraries of India and their Collections. p. 156-157
51. www.razalibrary.gov.nic.in
52. Annual Report 2004-05, Ministry of Culture, Government of India, p. 64.
53. www.razalibrary.gov.nic.in
54. Seventh Annual Report (2009-10) National Mission for Manuscripts.
55. Ibid.
56. Annual Report, 2004-05, Ministry of Culture, Government of India, pp. 35-36.
57. Raju, A.A.N., Documentary Heritage of Indian Libraries. p. 58-62.
58. Chapter VI, Ministry of Culture, Government of India.
59. Ibrahim Usmani. Salar Jung Museum to be digitized. February 1-15, 2005, Milli Gazette.
60. Report of the Working Group on Art and Culture for XI five Year Plan (2007-12) and Annual Plan (2007-08), Ministry of Culture, Government of India, January, 2007.
61. Seventh Annual Report (2009-10) National Mission for Manuscripts.
62. Chapter VI, Ministry of Culture, Government of India.
63. www.salarjungmuseum.in
64. Seventh Annual Report (2009-10) National Mission for Manuscripts.
65. Wikipedia: the free encyclopedia.
66. Ibid.

3

Contribution of National Mission for Manuscripts (Namami) in Preservation and Conservation of Oriental Heritage of India

Genesis and Development

The National Mission for Manuscripts was established in February 2003, by the Ministry of Tourism and Culture, Government of India. An ambitious project in its programme and mandate, the Mission seeks to unearth and preserve the vast manuscript wealth of India. India possesses an estimate of five million manuscripts, probably the largest collection in the world. These cover a variety of themes, textures and aesthetics, scripts, languages, calligraphies, illuminations and illustrations. Together, they constitute the 'memory' of India's history, heritage and thought. These manuscripts lie scattered across the country and beyond, in numerous institutions as well as private collections, often unattended and undocumented. The National Mission for Manuscripts aims to locate, document, preserve and render these accessible—to connect India's past with its future, its memory with its aspirations.

In the early 1980s, the Indira Gandhi National Centre for the Arts (IGNCA) took some steps towards rectifying the situation and carefully catalogued and micro-filmed about

1,00,000 important manuscripts around the country. Still, a major undertaking focused on manuscript conservation and documentation was missing. It was under the Tenth Five Year Plan that a sweeping initiative was announced. Working with specially identified Manuscript Resource Centres (MRCs) and Manuscript Conservation Centres (MCCs) in states all over the country, the Mission collects data on manuscripts located in a variety of places, from universities and libraries to Temples, Mathas, Madrasas, Monasteries and Private Collections. It also brings manuscripts and the knowledge they house to the public through lectures, seminars, publications and specially designed programmes for school children and university students. A number of other programmes are designed to promote manuscript conservation, manuscript digitization and scholarship through manuscript studies workshops.

The main objectives of the Mission include:

1. Locate manuscripts through national level Survey and Post-Survey
2. Conserve manuscripts incorporating both modern and indigenous methods of conservation and training a new generation of manuscript conservators
3. To train the next generation of scholars in various aspects of Manuscript Studies like languages, scripts and critical editing and cataloguing of texts and conservation of manuscripts
4. To promote access to manuscripts by digitizing the rarest and most endangered manuscripts
5. To promote access to manuscripts through publication of critical editions of unpublished manuscripts and catalogues.
6. To facilitate public's engagement with manuscripts through lectures, seminars, publications and other outreach programmes.

While doing an extra ordinary work on manuscripts, the Mission has been facing a few severe challenges since its very inception eight years back:

1. Very large collections of manuscripts in India estimate around 5 million.
2. Vast number of languages and scripts many of which can no longer be read.
3. Located in various kinds of repositories—ranging from museums, institutions of learning to private homes and houses of worship, big and small.
4. Found in very poor physical state-insect ridden, fungus infected or brittle, fading and fragile.
5. And finally, and perhaps most critically, there is a major lack of connection between so-called 'modern knowledge' and the knowledge contained in manuscripts. Scholars who can study and use manuscripts are fast disappearing and a new generation of scholars is not able to rise to the challenge.
6. Often, the knowledge in manuscripts is not seen as relevant to our times. Now that there is world-wide interest in traditional systems of medicine such as Ayurveda and Unani, building science such Vaastu Shasta and in older canons of literature and philosophy, there is revival of the search for manuscripts. But more importantly, manuscripts need to be saved for their importance as records of India's past, society, culture and politics—as records of India's memory.

National Database of Manuscripts : Since its very establishment, the Mission has done a remarkable progress in the direction of preserving and digitizing the vast collection of Indian manuscripts. In this direction, the Mission has launched the National Database of Manuscripts (Kritisampada) in the year 2007, which contains bibliographic information about more than one million texts. The Mission has not only included the institution of national importance, public and special libraries, monasteries, mathas, madrasas, mosques, temples but also individual collections to bring together information about over five million manuscripts of India which is perhaps highest in the World. It has documented and treated a number of manuscripts during last ten years duration.

Methodology of collecting Manuscripts: The Mission has formulated a systematic approach to collect the scattered manuscripts either preserves in the organisation or in the hands of individuals. The four most important methodologies which are being used to collect the relevant details about the manuscripts are worthy to discuss here:

7. **Survey and Post Survey:** It locates manuscripts in a house to house exercise through the national survey of manuscripts, carried out separately in each state. These manuscripts, once located, are documented in follow up post survey exercise wherein scholars are engaged to visit the repositories mapped in the survey. The post survey data accounts for the greatest percentage of data in the Kritisampada.
8. **Manuscript Resource Centres (MRCs):** These centres are scattered throughout the country from public institutions to private endowments. Spread across the Country, these centres engage scholars specifically for documentation of manuscripts in the Mission's format.
9. **Manuscript Partner Centres (MPCs):** The Mission's partners with institutes or private collections that have a very a large number of manuscripts or a very significant set of manuscripts to document each text in their ownership in the Mission's format.
10. **National Informatics Centre (NIC) and Indira Gandhi National Centre for Arts (IGNCA):** These centres are also helping in the creation of database in one or another way. The infrastructural support and manpower support given by NIC is tremendous. The software used by the Mission, developed by the NIC, is Manus Granthavali. It is updated frequently and has undergone several modifications with the additions of new fields' and the possibility of multiple subject entries for a single manuscript. Manus Granthavali is based on the Dublin Core Metadata Standards that are globally

accepted and used in the libraries everywhere. It is state-of-the-art Software having installed in almost all of the MRCs and MPCs of the Mission.

11. **Output:** Data is collected from various sources either in manually filled printed forms or in Compact Discs (CDs) containing electronic data collected and entered in the Computer by the MRCs and MPCs. The data is then subjected to screening, processing and editing at the mission's office in New Delhi before being entered into the Kritisampada. A systematic approach, knowledge of various scripts, languages and regional intellectual traditions are necessary to give shape to the final data. Therefore, Mission's personnel members in the Documentation Department are handpicked for the task and, between them, display a wide range of schololistc talent.

Till date, the Mission has utilising the services of following MRCs and MCCs throughout the Country:

Manuscript Resource Centres (MRC-s)

The National Mission for Manuscripts works with the help of 47 Manuscript Resource Centres across the country. These include wel-established Indological institutes, museums, libraries, universities and non-government organisations who act as the Mission's coordinating agency in their respective regions. They are primarily responsible for Survey and documentation of every manuscript in their area. The Mission liaises with them for awareness campaigns and outreach activities such as lectures, school theatre programme and training workshops.

Following are the list of institutions scattered throughout the country as Mission's MRC-s:

- Central Institute of Buddhist Studies, Leh
- Directorate of State Archaeology, Archives and Museum, Srinagar
- Himachal Academy of Arts, Culture and Languages, Shimla

- Library of Tibetan Works and Archives, Dharamsala
- Kurukshetra University, Kurukshetra
- Visweshvarananda Biswabandhu Institute of Sanskrit and Indological Studies, Hoshiarpur
- Uttaranchal Sanskrit Academy, Haridwaı
- Rampur Raza Library, Rampur
- Sampurnanand Sanskrit Visvavidyalaya, Varanasi
- Akhil Bhartiya Sanskrit Parishad, Lucknow
- H.N.B. Garhwal University, Pauri Garhwal, Uttaranchal
- Vrindavan Research Institute, Vrinadavan
- K. M. Hindi Institute of Hindi Studies and Linguistics, Agra
- Bhai Vir Singh Sahitya Sadan, New Delhi
- Institute of Tai Studies and Research, Moranhat, Assam
- B.L Institute of Indology, Delhi
- Mazahar Memorial Museum, Bahariabad, Ghazipur (UP)
- Oriental Research Institute, Sri Venkateswara University, Tirupati
- Andhra Pradesh Government Oriental Manuscripts Library and Research Institute, Hyderabad
- French Institute of Pondicherry, Pondicherry
- Department of Manuscriptology, Kannada University, Hampi
- National Institute of Prakrit Studies and Research, Shravanabelagola
- Keladi Museum and Historical Research Bureau, Shimoga
- Mahabharata Samshodhana Pratishthanam, Bangalore
- Thanjavur Maharaja Serfoji's Saraswati Mahal Library, Thanjavur
- University of Madras, Chennai
- Sri Oriental Research Institute and Manuscripts Library, University of Kerala, Thiruvananthapuram

- Chandra Sekharendra Saraswathi Viswa Mahavidyalaya, Kanchipuram
- Thunchan Memorial Trust, Tirur
- D.G, Centre for Heritage Studies,Thripunithura
- GOML & Research Centre University of Madras Library Campus, Chennai
- Khuda Bakhsh Oriental Public Library, Patna
- Kameshwar Singh Darbhanga Sanskrit University, Darbhanga
- Nava Nalanda Mahavihara, Nalanda, Bihar
- Sri D. K. Jain Oriental Research Institute, Arrah, Bihar
- Calcutta University Manuscripts Library, Kolkata
- Orissa State Museum, Bhubaneswar
- SARASVATI, Bhadrak
- Krishna Kanta Handiqui Library, Gauhati University, Guwahati
- Manipur State Archives, Imphal
- Gurucharan College, Silchar, Assam
- Culture and Archaeology Raipur (Chhatisgarh)
- Tripura University, Tripura
- Rajasthan Oriental Research Institute, Jodhpur
- Lalbhai Dalpatbhai Institute of Indology, Ahmedabad
- Bhandarkar Oriental Research Institute, Pune
- Kavikulaguru Kalidasa Sanskrit University, Ramtek
- Institute for Oriental Studies (Shiva Shakti), Thane
- Sat Shrut Prabhavana Trust, Bhavnagar
- Anandashram Sanstha, Pune
- Shree Dwarakadhish Sanskrit Academy and Indological Research Institute Dwaraka, Gujarat
- Shivaji University, Kolhapur
- Scindia Oriental Research Institute, Vikram University, Ujjain

- Dr. H. S. Gaur University, Sagar
- Kunda Kunda Jnanapitha, Indore

Manuscript Conservation Centres (MCC-s):

Following is the network of the MCC-s of the Mission throughout India:

- Central Institute of Buddhist Studies (CIBS), Leh
- Indira Gandhi National Centre for the Arts (IGNCA), New Delhi
- Department of Language and Culture, Shimla
- The Himalayan Society for Heritage and Art Conservation, Nainital
- Vrindavan Research Institute, Vrindavan
- Rampur Raza Library, Rampur
- Nagarjuna Buddhist Foundation, Gorakhpur
- Indian Conservation Institute, Lucknow
- Visweshvarananda Biswabandhu Institute of Sanskrit and Indological Studies, Hoshiarpur
- Central Library, Banaras Hindu University, Banaras
- B.L Institute of Indology, Delhi
- Kurukshetra University, Kurukshetra
- Mazahar Memorial Museum, Ghazipur
- Oriental Research Institute, Sri Venkateswara University, Tirupati
- Salar Jung Museum, Hyderabad
- INTACH Chitrakala Parishath Art Conservation Centre, Bangalore
- Tamil Nadu Government Museum, Chennai
- Karnataka State Archives, Bangalore
- Tanjore Maharaja Serfoji's Saraswati Mahal Library, Thanjavur
- Mural Painting Conservation Research and Training Centre, Trippunithura Palace, Cochin

- Regional Conservation Laboratory, Thiruvananthapuram
- A P State Archives and Research Institute, Hydrabad
- Kannada University, Hampi
- National Institute of Prakrit Studies and Research, Srovanabelagola
- Keladi Museum and Historical Research, Keladi
- Thunchan Memorial Trust, Tirur
- Centre for Heritage Studies, Thripunithura
- ORI and Manuscripts Library, Trivandrum
- Khuda Bakhsh Oriental Public Library, Patna
- Sri Dev Kumar Jain Oriental research Institute, Arrah
- Manuscript Library, University of Calcutta, Kolkata
- INTACH Orissa Art Conservation Centre, Bhubaneswar
- AITIHYA, Bhubaneswar
- Sambalpur University, Burla, Orissa
- Krishna Kanta Handiqui Library, Gauhati University, Guwahati
- Manipur State Archives, Imphal
- Tawang Monastery, Tawang
- Gurucaharan College, Silchar
- Patna Museum, Patna
- Culture and Archaeology, Raipur
- Orissa State Museum, Bhubaneswar
- Tripura University, Tripura
- Rajasthan Oriental Research Institute, Jodhpur
- Mahaveer Digamber Jain Pandulipi Samrakshan Kendra, Jaipur, Rajasthan
- Lalbhai Dalpatbhai Institute of Indology, Ahmedabad
- Bhandarkar Oriental Research Institute (BORI), Pune
- Scindia Oriental Research Institute (SORI), Ujjain
- Kund Kund Jananpith, Indore

Merits of Database

The Database created by the Mission has following key elements:

- Mainly, it has been divided into two main search options namely regions wise and category wise.
- Further, it has a number of options through which the required manuscripts can be searched. These are:
  - Title
  - Subject
  - Author
  - Language
  - Script
  - Material
  - State
- The software is in bilingual and provides entries in English and Hindi.
- Transliteration method has been applied while giving information about the non English manuscripts excluding Hindi.
- Till date, it has covered 24 states of India for providing bibliographic data of manuscripts in their various organisations.
- The database contains a vast number of Indian languages through which anybody can search the entire collections.
- Contains manuscripts of renowned libraries, academic institutions, and religious places besides many personal collections.

Demerits of Database

The following demerits/mistakes found in the Database that should be rectified as early as possible:

- The details of oriental language manuscripts should be available in the specific language in which the manuscript originally produced.

- The Telugu manuscripts of APGOMLRI, Hyderabad got place in the Mission's Database but other language manuscripts such as Urdu, Arabic and Persian could not uploaded, which constitutes almost 75% of its treasure wealth.
- Though, a number of small libraries/institutes got place in its database from the state of Jammu and Kashmir, but, it is strange that, the Central Institute of Budhist Studies, Leh, Ladakh, could not occupy information regarding its manuscripts wealth in the Database.
- A number of typographical mistakes especially in the bibliographic details of the Oriental language manuscripts found in the Database, which should be rectified.
- A number of times, several elements regarding the details of manuscripts either not visible or written in some meaningless codes. The authorities should take note of these mistakes and the same will be corrected as soon as possible.
- A few states of India do not occupy their place the Mission's Database though they are having important organisation/ libraries which are specialized in oriental language documents.

4

Summary and Conclusions

Introduction

A comprehensive study on the vast topic of oriental libraries with respect to establishment, collection development and modernization is a very tedious task. Due to huge collection and their background, it is not possible to cover each and every aspects related to these libraries. The most important aspects of the study to identify where these libraries are standing and how much their access to masses is compatible with modern fruits of Information Technology. Change is the law of nature and if these valuable libraries have to survive, these have to change not only their outlook but also accessibility. They have to utilize every fruit of Information Technology. With the help and assistance of various outcome of ICT, these libraries have to implement not only necessary infrastructure but also personnel; those make them real virtual digital organizations compatible with foreign and developed nations. Only through digitization, these organizations can make a better place in the vast changing environment.

Though, most of Indian oriental public libraries have started to transform their invaluable collection of old volumes and rare manuscripts into digital format, but few are lagging behind. There is need to speed up their digitization process. In this direction, the support of the government organizations and NGO are very crucial. In this section, while concluding the discussion, it seems feasible to provide few important statistics about the above libraries for a bird eye view.

S. No.	*Name of organization (Acronym)*	*Year of origin*	*No. of Books (Approx)*	*No. of MSS (Approx)*	*Website / URL*	*Auto-mated*	*Digi-tized*	*OPAC / Web OPAC*
01.	APGOMLRI, Hyderabad	1967	7,876	24,040	www.manuscriptlibrary.ap.nic.in	–	Started	
02.	ASL, Kolkata	1784	1,49,000	47,000	www.asiaticsocietycal.com	–	–	--
03.	ASM, Mumbai	1804	--	3,000	www.asiaticsocietymumbai.org	Yes	--	Web OPAC
04.	BORI, Pune	1917	1,25,000	29,510	www.bori.ac.in	–	Started in 2003	–
05.	CIBS, Leh	1959	28,000	10,000	www.cibsleh.in	–	--	–
06.	CPL, Chennai	1890	6,36,000	--	www.connemarapubliclibrarychennai.com	yes	–	Web OPAC
07.	DMSA, Azamgarh	1914	1,00,000	650	www.shibliacademy.org	–	--	–
08.	DUNU, Lucknow	1894	1,50,000	----	www.nadwatululama.org	yes	--	--
09.	GOML&RC, Chennai	1869	25,373	72,314	www.telupu.com/goml	---	--	--
10.	HPMSL, Ahmadabad	--	10,000	2,000	----	--	--	--
11.	KBOPL, Patna	1891	2,50,000	21,000	www.kblibrary.bih.nic.in	yes	Started	Web OPAC

S. No.	Name of organization (Acronym)	Year of origin	No. of Books (Approx)	No. of MSS (Approx)	Website / URL	Auto-mated	Digitized	OPAC / Web OPAC
14.	MSSML, Thanjavur	1918	52,094	47,625	www.sarasvatimahallibrary.tn.nic.in	yes	Started in 2003	—
15.	NL, Kolkata	1948	24,02,57 9	3,227	www.nationallibrary.org	yes	Started in 1990	Web OPAC
16.	RRL, Rampur	1774	80,000	15,000	www.razalibrary.gov.in	yes	Started in 2003	Web OPAC
17.	SDKJORI, Arrah	1903	9,000	6679	www.jainmanuscripts.nic.in	—	---	—
18.	SJML, Hyderabad	1951	57,882	9,000	www.salarjungmuseum.in	—	Started in 2005	—
19.	SORI, Ujjain	1957	---	18,695	—	—	—	—

Source: websites of Libraries,2011 and other relevant Secondary Source

Findings and Observations

During the course of study, the writer has made an attempt to minutely study, explore, relate and analyze various measures taken by these libraries to modernize their activities as well as accessibility for its clienteles. Their existence is also interdependent upon their modernization of collections and services. The development of the study has made an impact on the researcher's mind; and has led to various findings and observations, of which major ones are reported as follows:

- Most of the chosen oriental libraries of India possess huge collection of printed documents as well as manuscripts which are very useful for researchers and scholars.
- Most of these libraries have made modest attempt to modernize their collection and services, but their speed is very slow.
- The data about the collection of printed documents and manuscripts of these originations provided in articles/ books varies considerably from author to author.
- The language wise break up of documents housed by these organisations either not known or not up-to-date in most of the above mentioned libraries.
- Though, most of these organisations have their own websites but only a few of them made an effort to display their particular OPACs on Net.
- Some of the selected libraries are doing very good effort as far as digitization of their manuscripts is concerned.
- A number of chosen libraries are serving as nodal centers for 'National Mission for Manuscripts' which is a national level agency strived for proper preservation and digitization of manuscripts treasures.
- There is a need to frame some standard policy for digitization of manuscripts preserved in Indian libraries; both public and academic libraries possessing very strong collection in oriental language manuscripts.

- Every effort has done to make possible all the recommendations made by National Knowledge Commission of India (NKC).
- Effort should be made to acquire manuscripts on oriental languages, literature and culture from private small libraries and individuals and make them accessible to users by transforming them into digitized format.
- Scanning based digitization should be avoided atleast in the case of old and brittle documents, unless other media failed to do so.
- The libraries should be provided with huge grants by the central government as well as state governments for purchase of sophisticated tools for digitization.
- There is also, an urgent need to make available their Online Public Access Catalogue (OPAC) on their particular websites from the part of concerned organizations.
- There is urgent need to rectify the typographical and other errors in the Manuscripts Database being developed by the National Mission for Manuscripts.
- The Mission will also include the remaing states of India such as Arunachal Pradesh, Goa etc in its Database.
- While putting the data of Arabic, Persian and Urdu manuscripts, the Mission should take the help of experts in thses languages.

Implications of the Study

The main implication of this study is to understand their place in the era of Information and Communications Technology (ICT). It is also envisage that, these libraries still have to play a very crucial role in the modern research. The treasures of these libraries accompanied with invaluable and rare manuscripts are always needed by the scholars and intellectuals who want to pursue rigorous fundamental research on Indian Ancient and Medieval history including history of South East Asia. These treasures trove of knowledge are the basis of any fundamental research. The study undertaken may encourage other scholars to pursue further researches on these libraries from various other angles.

Scope for Future Work

The study has open doors for further research on these or other libraries of same category from various perspectives. There is still need to elaborate detailed description on their manuscripts treasures. The importance of these libraries lies in their collection of valuable and rare manuscripts, therefore, a study can be taken in future to explore while providing abstracts of each manuscripts in English language. Manuscripts and rare documents stored in these libraries are valuable assets; therefore, there is always novelty in doing research in these areas.

Select Bibliography

1. Amjad Ali, Oriental Libraries and their Collections, 2004, Ess Ess, New Delhi.
2. Raju, A.A.N., Documentary Heritage of Indian Libraries. 2003, Ess Ess, New Delhi.
3. Vasantha, N and Mahesh V. Mudhol, Software Packages for Automation.2000, Ess Ess, New Delhi.
4. Kumar, P.S.G., Computerization of Indian Libraries.1987, B.R.Publishing Corporation, Delhi
5. Jain, M.K. and Jain, Nirmal, Teaching-Learning Library and Information Services: A Manual. 2006, Shipra, New Delhi.
6. http://kblibrary.bih.nic.in
7. http://nlindia.org
8. http://namami.nic.in
9. http://dli.ernet.in
10. http://www.vidyanidhi.org.in
11. http://www.asiaticsocietycal.com
12. http://www.sarasvatimahallibrary.tn.nic.in
13. http://www.salarjungmuseum.in
14. http://www.connemarapubliclibrarychennai.com
15. http://www.bori.ac.in
16. http://www.ltwa.net
17. http://www.telupu.com/GOML
18. http://www.razalibrary.gov.in

19. Kalpana Dasgupta, Digitization, Sustainability and Access in Indian Context. IFLA, 2005, Oslo.
20. Amjad Ali, Digital Libraries and Information Networks, 2007, Ess Ess, New Delhi.
21. Arms, William Y., Digital Libraries. 2000, MIT Press, Cambridge.
22. Waters Donald. J., What are Digital Libraries? CLIR, July/ August, 1998.
23. Parvathamma, N., Digital Divide in India; Need for correcting Bias (Communications).Information Technology and Libraries.
24. Madalli, Devika P., A Digital Library of Library and Information Science using D-Space, Paper presented at DRTC Workshop on Semantic Web, Bangalore, India, 8-10 December, 2003.
25. Witten, I.H. and Bainbridge, D., Practical Digital Library Interoperability Standards, Proceedings of the 5th ACM/ IEEE-CS Joint Conference on Digital Libraries.
26. Sreekumar, M.G. et al., Institutional Repositories for Knowledge Management in Academic and Research Institutions, International Conference on Semantic Web and Digital Libraries.
27. Tyagi, Shashi et. al. (Ed), Digitization and Digital Preservation. Conference papers, 11-12 December, 2008, DESIDOC, New Delhi.
28. http://www.infolibrarian.com/
29. http://www.openarchives.org/
30. http://www.niscair.res.in
31. http://www.nalanda.nic.ac.in
32. http://www.drtc.isibang.ac.in
33. http://www. tifr.res.in
34. http://www\vidyanidhi.org.in
35. http://emeraldinsight.com

36. http://www.indiaedu.com/libraries
37. http://www.indiafocus.indiainfo.com/media/library
38. http://www.nigd.org/libraries
39. http://www.en.wikipedia.org/wiki/National-library-of-india
40. http://www.indialibraries.blogspot.com
41. http://www.accessmylibrary.com
42. http://www.kar.nic.in/publib
43. http://www.webpages.uidaho.edu/embolin/wani
44. http://www.encyclopedia.com/doc
45. http://www.ajayshagblog.blogspot.com
46. http://www.lib.unc.edu
47. http://www.ifap-is-observatory.ittk
48. http://www.surfindia.com/education/library
49. http://www.diglib.org/about/dldefinition.html
50. A concise descriptive catalogue of the Persian manuscripts in Salar Jung Museum and Library, Hyderabad. Compiled by Muhammad Ashraf. 12 Vols, Hyderabad, SJML. (vol.1:1965, vol.2:1966, vol.3: 1966, vol. 4: 1967, vol. 5: 1969, vol. 6: 1975, vol. 7: 1980, vol. 8: 1983, vol. 9: 1988, vol. 10: 1991, vol. 11: 1997, vol. 12: 2007).
51. A catalogue of the rabic manuscripts in Salar Jung Museum and Library. Compiled by Muhammad Ashraf. 8 Vols. Hyderabad, SJML. (vol. 1: 1957, vol. 2: 1962, vol. 3: 1978, vol. 4: 1981, vol. 5: 1986, vol. 6: 1989, vol. 7: 1993, vol. 8: 2000).
52. Kutubkhana Nawab Salar Jung Marhoom ki Urdu kitabon ki Wazahati Fihrist. Compiled by Hashmi, Naseeruddin. Hyderabad, SJML, 1957.
53. A. descriptive catalogue of Urdu manuscripts (Poetry). Compiled by Rafat Rizwana. Vols.1, APGOMLRI, Hyderabad, 1988.
54. A descriptive catalogue of Urdu manuscripts (Poetry). Compiled by Rafat Rizwana. Vols. 2, APGOMLRI, Hyderabad, 1994.

55. Fihrist Mashruh Baaz Kutub Nafsiyah Qalmiyah Makhzoon Kutubkhana Asafiya Sarker-e-Aali. Vol.2. Darut Taba Sarkar-e-Aali, Hyderbad, 1357 A.H.

56. Hand Book of Andhra Pradesh Government Oriental Manuscripts Library and Research Institute. Compiled by V.V.L. Narsimha Rao and V. Sarala Kumari. APGOMLRI, Hyderabad, 1988.

57. Amjad Ali, Oriental Manuscripts Worldwide, 2005, Ess Ess, New Delhi.

58. Catalogue of Persian manuscripts in buhar collection. Vol. 1. 1982, National Library, Kolkata.

59. Gupta, B.M., Handbook of Libraries, Archives and Information Centers in India. 2003, Scientific Publishers, Jodhpur.

60. Khan, Shaukat Ali. Historical Heritage: A bibliographical survey of the rare manuscripts. 1980, MAAPRI, Tonk.

61. O, Connor Scott, V.C. An Eastern Library: An introduction to the Khuda BakhshLibrary, 1991, Ed. 2, Maktaba Jamia, New Delhi.

62. Nadwi, Salman Shamsi. Hindustan key Mashriqi Kutub Khaney, 1973, Center for Publications and Studies, Lucknow.

63. Abidi, Raza Ali. Kutub Khana. 1994, Educational Book House, Aligarh.

64. Information Sources, Systems and Programmes. MLIS-02, IGNOU Course Material for MLIS students.

65. http://sarn.saarc.org/libraries

Index